RAND NATIONAL DEFENSE RESEARCH INSTITUTE

SURPRISE!

From CEOs to Navy SEALs:
How a Select Group of Professionals Prepare
for and Respond to the Unexpected

Dave Baiocchi · D. Steven Fox

D0701540

Prepared for the National Reconnaissance Office

The research described in this report was prepared for the National Reconnaissance Office. The research was conducted within the RAND National Defense Research Institute, a federally funded research and development center sponsored by the Office of the Secretary of Defense, the Joint Staff, the Unified Combatant Commands, the Navy, the Marine Corps, the defense agencies, and the defense Intelligence Community under Contract NRO-000-12-C-0187.

Library of Congress Cataloging-in-Publication Data

Baiocchi, Dave.
  Surprise! : from CEOs to Navy Seals : how a select group of professionals prepare for and respond to the unexpected / Dave Baiocchi, D. Steven Fox.
      pages cm
  Includes bibliographical references.
  ISBN 978-0-8330-8103-2 (pbk. : alk. paper)
  1. Emergency management. 2. Surprise. I. Fox, D. Steven. II. Title.

  HD49.B337 2013
  658.4'0354—dc23

                                                                    2013030891

RAND OFFICES
SANTA MONICA, CA • WASHINGTON, DC
PITTSBURGH, PA • NEW ORLEANS, LA • JACKSON, MS • BOSTON, MA
DOHA, QA • CAMBRIDGE, UK • BRUSSELS, BE
www.rand.org

Preface

The objective of this research was to investigate how a variety of professions prepare for and respond to surprise. After speaking with former ambassadors, chief executive officers, military personnel, and health care professionals (among others), we report on some common methods and techniques that they use to prepare for and respond to unforeseen situations. We focused on two factors that influence how practitioners deal with surprise—available response time and level of chaos in the work environment—and we note how these factors affect people's approaches toward preparing for and responding to unexpected events.

We performed this research for the Advanced Systems & Technologies Directorate (AS&T) at the National Reconnaissance Office (NRO). The NRO faces an operational environment that is faster paced, more uncertain, and filled with more variables than it was even ten years ago. One of the biggest challenges facing the Intelligence Community today is that it must confront unknown threats that continue to emerge from unexpected directions. To address these challenges, the NRO asked RAND to investigate how other occupations prepare for and respond to unexpected events (surprises). For example: Are there practices that medical practitioners, military personnel, or foreign service workers employ that could teach AS&T something about how to better prepare for unexpected events? The findings from this research will therefore be useful to NRO strategists as they make plans to shape the workforce and future operations.

This research was conducted within the Intelligence Policy Center of the RAND National Security Research Division (NSRD). NSRD conducts research and analysis on defense and national security topics for the U.S. and allied defense, foreign policy, homeland security, and intelligence communities and foundations and other nongovernmental organizations that support defense and national security analysis.

For more information on the Intelligence Policy Center, see http://www.rand.org/nsrd/ndri/centers/intel.html or contact the director (contact information is provided on the web page).

Contents

Figures and Tables

Figures

Tables

Summary

Nearly all professionals—including laborers, knowledge workers, and policymakers—must deal with the unexpected. Indeed, many organizations face an operational environment that is faster paced, more uncertain, and filled with more variables than it was even ten years ago. Some professionals must respond to changes in their environment quickly—sometimes instantaneously—which makes planning for the unexpected of critical importance.

Anecdotal evidence suggests that people in different occupations respond to unexpected situations, or surprises, in different ways. For example, every National Football League (NFL) coach develops a "playbook" that aims to catalogue and have a play ready for every possible situation that might occur during a game. In other words, the coach deals with the unexpected by trying to prevent surprises from being "surprises" at all. In contrast, a Navy Sea, Air, Land (SEAL) special forces member cannot possibly anticipate every type of situation that might occur in a military operating environment and therefore cannot catalogue all the "what if" scenarios. Instead, the SEAL prepares for the unexpected by focusing on important but broad parameters relevant to every mission: What is the mission goal? What is the route to the target? What are the primary threats the team is likely to face?

Such observations provoked questions about how different professions prepare for and respond to surprise, as well as an interest in deriving lessons on how professionals of all sorts can become more adept at planning for an uncertain future. This report represents an investigation into what diverse professionals believe creates surprise, how they respond to it, and how the effects of surprise can be mitigated.

To explore these issues, we explored existing literature on decisionmaking, used this material as context for developing a framework for thinking about how different professionals respond to surprise, and conducted discussions with a wide variety of professionals. (We have refrained from disclosing the names of persons with whom we spoke because part of our research approach was to promise participants anonymity to ensure their candor.) In our discussions, we asked questions that sought to highlight the techniques and tools each person relies on when responding to surprise.

Thinking About the Unexpected

To understand how people in different professions address surprise, we first categorized three types of "surprise encounters" faced by different professions. For example, some "high stakes" professionals, such as trauma surgeons, firefighters, and military special forces, regularly face unexpected situations with the potential for profound—often life-or-death—consequences. In comparison, a very large set of "quick tempo" professionals, including chefs, stock traders, professional coaches, and theatrical performers, operate in a fast-paced environment that includes many unexpected, but not typically life-threatening, events. Finally, "knowledge worker" professionals, such as chief executive officers (CEOs), politicians, and foreign service officers, may face surprises less frequently than some other occupations; however, decisions made and activities taken by these professions to respond to the unexpected can have profound long-term effects on the world economy, environment, and political situation. Table S.1 shows example occupations for each of these categories.

A Framework for Understanding How Different Professions Respond to Surprise

As we considered the differences in the ways that various occupations address the unexpected, we developed a framework for understanding

Table S.1.
Categories of Occupations and Example Professions

High-Stakes, Fast-Paced	Moderate-Stakes, Fast-Paced	Longer-Term Decisionmaking
Trauma surgeons	Improv actors	Diplomats
Emergency room physicians	Taxi drivers	Foreign service officers
Firefighters	Flight attendants	Military general officers
Combat pilots	Photojournalists	Space mission commanders
Arctic fishermen	PR officers	Civil engineers
Military special forces	Stock traders	Trial attorneys
Extreme skiers	Professional coaches	Politicians
Hostage negotiators	Chefs	C-level executives
SWAT team commanders		

how different professions respond to surprise. The framework recognizes that different professions' responses to surprise vary according to two key factors: *the time available to respond to an unexpected event and the level of chaos in the environment.* For example, some occupations, such as medical practitioners and military personnel, have to respond to an unexpected event within minutes or seconds while others, such as ambassadors and CEOs, might wait hours, days, or weeks before having to respond. Further, some professionals operate within highly controlled environments (such as a sports venue), while others, such as Navy SEALs, operate in an environment that includes a large number of factors over which the professional has little control (e.g., colleagues, terrain, weather, adversary movement, equipment, civilians), thus leading to a higher potential for chaos, the number of unknowns, and complicating variables.

Figure S.1 shows how we categorized different types of professions according to these two variables, *typical response time* and *level of chaos in the environment*, which are shown along the horizontal and vertical axes, respectively. Representatives from all the professions in the figure were included in the interviews for this research.

The framework allows us to make some observations about different types of professions. For example, the professions shown on the left side of Figure S.1 tend to be more *tactical* (i.e., involving touch labor, hand-eye coordination, physical activity), while the professions

Figure S.1
A Framework for Understanding How Different Professionals Respond to Surprise

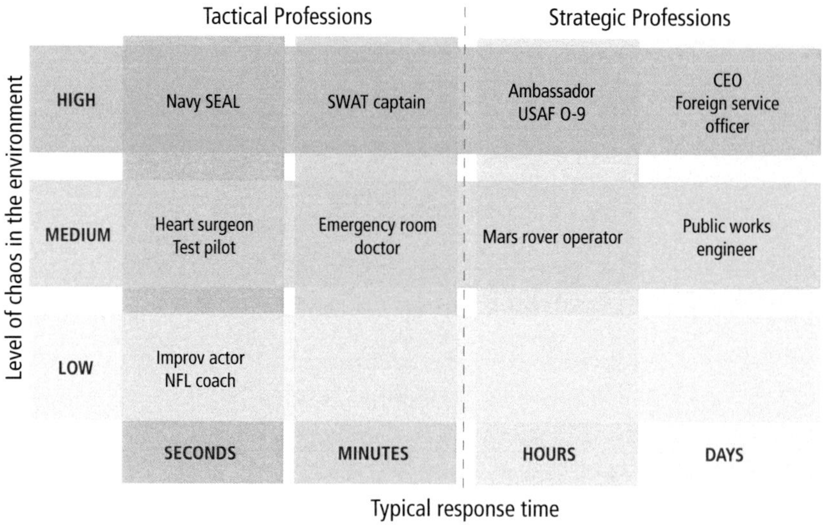

		Tactical Professions		Strategic Professions	
HIGH	Navy SEAL	SWAT captain	Ambassador USAF O-9	CEO Foreign service officer
MEDIUM	Heart surgeon Test pilot	Emergency room doctor	Mars rover operator	Public works engineer
LOW	Improv actor NFL coach			
	SECONDS	MINUTES	HOURS	DAYS

Level of chaos in the environment

Typical response time

RAND RR341-S.1

on the right tend to be more *strategic* (i.e., involving knowledge capital). Figure S.1 can also be read from top to bottom. The professions experiencing the highest level of chaos (top row of the figure) tend to face surprises generated by other humans, while professions working in moderate- or low-chaos environments (lower portions of the figure) face surprises that are generated primarily by environmental factors.

Key Findings

Our methods for generating hypotheses and collecting data are described in detail in the main body of this report. The conclusions that we note below are based on data from a small set of interviews from exemplar professions, and there is always a danger of drawing a false conclusion from scanty data. Our main objective was to identify general trends across the professions and our discussions were sufficient in meeting that goal. As our series of interviews progressed, we started to hear familiar narratives repeated, which was a good indication that we were reaching the point where conducting additional interviews would yield diminishing returns. Therefore, the observations and key findings that we describe below are based on our interviews with a limited set of professions, and the statements that we make are in relation to the group of practitioners we interviewed.

Is There a Set of Common Response Techniques Across Professions?
We identified four strategies that were common across all of the professionals we interviewed. First, we observed that they *rely on experience* when dealing with surprise. Experience is one of the best insurance policies against the negative effects of surprise because it allows people to recognize what is happening during the unexpected event and thus to respond earlier and more effectively. We also observed that they *try to reduce the level of chaos in their operating environment*, since reducing chaos also reduces the complexity and scope of the solution space. In practice, we found that professionals reduce chaos by eliminating as many variables as possible by fixing their values. We learned that they *try to use a measured response to surprise* (e.g., by keeping over-confidence and emotions in check, allocating resources in a measured way), which helps keep response options open as the surprise unfolds. Finally, we found that everyone we interviewed *values teamwork when responding to unexpected events*, including professions that some may imagine as "individually focused" professions, such as heart surgeons or test pilots.[1] All types of professionals rely on colleagues to help plan and prepare for surprise, scan for and report surprises when they occur, and refine and execute the response following a surprise.

Do Tactical Professions Respond to Surprise Differently Than Strategic Professions?
There were, however, important differences in the response approaches taken by those involved in tactical professions (e.g., medical practitio-

---

[1]   As we describe later in the text, the imagery of a heart surgeon or test pilot working alone was a misconception on our part—a fact that we later discovered and corrected after speaking with the practitioners.

ners, Special Weapons and Tactics [SWAT] team members) and those involved in strategic professions (e.g., CEOs, foreign service officers).

First, strategists generally have to work harder than tacticians to identify and react to surprise. Generally speaking, strategic professionals have relatively more time to respond to surprises and often rely on others to detect and identify them. Thus, communication and coordination—though important for most professions—are particularly critical for strategists, who will typically use these approaches often and earlier in the response process.

Second, strategists tend to use a different response loop than do tacticians. Tactical professionals must often overcome emotions of fear and panic in order to successfully deal with a surprise. In contrast, strategists must work to contain anger and impulsive desires to overreact. We observed that tacticians typically rely on protocols to overcome panic and respond effectively using minimal analysis. A common tactical protocol involves three steps: 1) control panic; 2) buy time; and 3) revert to fundamentals learned in training and through prior experience. In contrast, successful strategists tend to use a four-step process to control emotion and facilitate teamwork: 1) control emotion and possible overconfidence; 2) initiate first-order steps to start the response; 3) convene a trusted inner circle of advisers and direct reports; and 4) disseminate a coherent longer-term response throughout the organization.

How Does Environmental Chaos Affect the Way Professionals Prepare for and Respond to Surprise?

We found that the level of environmental chaos strongly affects the way in which different professions prepare for and respond to surprise. Our interviews revealed four key insights.

In less-chaotic (and more-controllable) environments, professionals rely more on "what if" response plans that are thought out in advance, while in more-complex environments, professionals develop general response frameworks that are useful in a variety of situations. Professionals who work in the most-contrived (low-chaos) environments, such as athletic fields, face only a finite range of possible surprises and outcomes and thus are typically better able to plan a response for nearly any event, as NFL coaches regularly do. Professionals who work in moderately chaotic environments like operating rooms or test plane cockpits rely on pre-planned protocols for the most likely events, as well as for some less common, but possible, surprises. However, there are too many unforeseen events in moderately chaotic environments to plan against every possibility, so these professionals also employ some basic response frameworks that they can fall back on if the surprise event is not covered by a more specific protocol.

The most challenging circumstances are faced by those who work in highly chaotic environments, such as a foreign embassy or behind enemy lines. Such environments can be so complex and unpredictable that it does not make sense to do much planning against specific surprise events. Instead, these professions develop and exercise a more general-purpose framework, or series of steps, that can be deployed whenever a major surprise is encountered.

The most complex and chaotic situations are caused by other humans, rather than solely by environmental factors. While the environment can introduce a wide range of factors that contribute to the level of chaos in unexpected situations, the actions of other humans are typically involved in the most-chaotic situations. Human actions are often unpredictable, especially when a large number of people interact with each other. When people are at the root of a surprise, the level of complexity increases, and this dramatically magnifies the difficulty of developing specific response plans ahead of time.

Once a surprise occurs, an effective response depends more on whether the surprise is *recognized* or *unrecognized*, not whether it is *known* or *unknown*. In moderate and highly chaotic environments, a key challenge is often to understand, or *recognize*, what is happening when a surprise occurs. That is, the range of possibilities is generally known, but the challenge is to recognize the features of a particular situation as it is happening. Once the nature of a surprise is recognized as something similar to what the practitioner has experienced previously, the response can be focused and precise (either a specific plan worked out in advance or the appropriate general response strategy), whereas the response to an unrecognized situation must be more tentative and generic.

A surprise caused by other humans most often comes from a third party, not a known adversary. For professionals in the most chaotic environments, their biggest surprises arise from the actions of a third party (e.g., a bystander, a civilian in a military environment) rather than a direct adversary or stakeholder. The intuitive explanation for this phenomenon is that people usually have a good understanding of their most direct threats; i.e., they understand the calculus that drives adversary or stakeholder behavior and can make appropriate plans to avert or respond to surprise. However, despite such preparations, professionals can still be open and vulnerable to less predictable third-party actions, even when that third party has no adversarial intent.

Recommendations

Our findings generated several recommendations on how professionals can prepare for and respond to surprise:

Learn from experience: Attract and retain the most experienced people. Nearly everyone told us that nothing substitutes for experience. Practically speaking, this means that teams and organizations seeking to minimize surprise also need to attract and retain the most experienced people, since they represent an organization's best general defense against surprise.

Address the negative effects of surprise. Professionals in any field can take additional steps to mitigate the negative effects of surprise, including:

- fostering collaborative tools that help share knowledge and experience across an organization
- developing mechanisms to encourage measured responses
- instilling the workforce with the mind-set that surprises can often be converted into both opportunities and learning experiences.

Assess the level of chaos in the work environment. Professionals who work in more contrived environments are typically able to develop a plan for most contingencies, and should devote most of their energy toward developing more-comprehensive response plans. Those professionals working in moderately or highly chaotic environments should develop specific response plans that focus on the most likely surprises and existential threats. They should also develop and exercise more generalized response frameworks to use when an unrecognized surprise occurs.

Prepare for "third-party surprises." While most tacticians probably do not engage in "alternative futures" exercises, they can benefit from the philosophy associated with those events. Toward that end, all professionals should spend part of their planning time specifically thinking about threats or surprises that could originate from outside their usual field of view. It may be helpful to engage a third party in this exercise to further expand the scope.

Beyond these broad suggestions, our findings also suggest some lessons targeted at strategic occupations.

Focus on building a network of trusted colleagues. Strategic professionals are often in charge of large groups of people or whole organizations, and therefore tend to be more reliant on a team approach to both detect and handle their surprises. Successful strategists therefore benefit from a network of trusted colleagues at all levels of the organization. This network can also function as "surprise sensors," greatly expanding the chief strategist's field of view.

Conduct regular future-planning exercises. Strategists can gain significant benefit from conducting regular exercises to identify alternative futures. When conducting these exercises, strategists should instruct the participants to adopt an open perspective and a very wide field of view, not focusing solely on known stakeholders, competitors, and adversaries, but also potential actions by third parties. While the exercise should seek to prepare for a large set of possible threats, the act of identifying all potential sources of surprise alone represents an important step toward mitigating the possible effects of surprise.

Acknowledgements

We are very grateful for our sponsors at the National Reconnaissance Office, Advanced Systems and Technology Directorate, Robert Brodowski and Susan Durham, who have been helpful and supportive of this work from the start. We are also thankful for the guidance that we received from Geoffrey Torrington. It was Geoff who first inspired us to consider what the Intelligence Community could learn about becoming more flexible by looking at other professions.

We are very grateful for all of the expert practitioners with whom we spoke for this project. Everyone we approached was not only willing to share his or her experience, they all were also unstinting with their time and insight. Their thoughtful perceptions taught us a tremendous amount about how to approach surprise. We could not have done this project without them, and we offer them all a sincere thank you for giving us such a clear view into their complex professional worlds.

We are also very thankful for several colleagues, both inside and outside of RAND Corporation. At the very beginning, Steve Rast from the Aerospace Corporation contributed some key insights that eventually led us to our framework. Bill Welser IV kept us on track by participating in the discussions that generated and refined our initial framework. Andrew Weiss helped us establish connections with former Department of State personnel. Scott Savitz, Carol "Rollie" Flynn, Matt Lewis, Tim Webb, and Melissa Bradley read early drafts of this work and provided critical feedback that made the report stronger and more compelling. Amy McGranahan worked hard at assembling the initial manuscript, and we appreciate all of the day-to-day support that she provided throughout this project. Finally, we appreciate the efforts of our editing team: Kristin Leuschner, Arwen Bicknell, Matt Byrd, and Steve Kistler. All of these individuals worked hard to make sure this piece was properly edited and visually attractive. The observations and conclusions made within this report are solely those of the authors, as are any errors or omissions, and do not represent the official views or policies of the U.S. Intelligence Community or of the RAND Corporation.

Abbreviations

AS&T	Advanced Systems and Technology Directorate
CEO	chief executive officer
FMEA	failure modes and effects analysis
HRO	high-reliability organization
IC	Intelligence Community
JPL	Jet Propulsion Laboratories
KU	known unknown
NFL	National Football League
NRO	National Reconnaissance Office
RPD	recognition-primed decision
SEAL	Sea, Air, Land (U.S. Navy special forces team member)
SWAT	Special Weapons and Tactics (team)
UU	unknown unknown

CHAPTER ONE

Introduction

It is hard to surprise Mike Wheaton.[1] A National Football League (NFL) coach for more than 20 years, Wheaton is one of the longest-serving coaches in franchise history. Over the span of his career, he has seen it all, including the time an opposing team punted the football in the middle of a blizzard, and the ball landed *behind* the punter for a loss of several yards. In a sport known for short-lived careers, Wheaton's long tenure is a testament to his effectiveness: His job was to prepare his team so they would never be surprised by an opponent on game day.

To achieve that goal, Wheaton began every preseason by reviewing his team's upcoming game schedule. He would consider the opposing coaching staffs and look at decisions they had made in previous seasons. He would review hundreds of hours of video along with photographs of every formation from every game. He would calculate relative probabilities of how his opponents would likely behave in any scenario, and he built response plans based on those assumptions.

The product of all of this preparation was his team's playbook, which served as his how-to manual for preventing surprise. It contained prescribed reactions to every scenario Wheaton could imagine the team might encounter during a game, and it was so extensive that it contained a response for every combination of opponent formation, field position, and down number. The coaching staff would feed these

---

[1] To preserve the anonymity of our practitioners, we have changed the names and genericized the job titles of individuals described throughout this piece.

variables into the playbook, and it would return a reaction plan for any scenario.

Wheaton's job was to envision everything that could happen to the team and devise a reaction to it. In preparing all these reactions, he significantly reduced the chances that his team would ever encounter the unexpected. By doing a lot of up-front planning, Wheaton was able to minimize any negative risk associated with surprises. In fact, his relationship with surprise was summed up by a statement he made to us at the very beginning of our discussion: "If I'm doing my job right, there shouldn't be any surprises."[2] But what about practitioners who do not possess the luxury of a planning season and reams of historical performance data?

At first glance, it would seem that former Navy Sea, Air, Land (SEAL) special forces member Chris Bradford would appreciate Wheaton's approach to dealing with surprise. Bradford, who served as the platoon commander for a Navy SEAL team, was in the business of creating surprises for his adversaries. As Bradford notes, SEAL teams are small and nimble so they are not in a position of overwhelming their opponents with a large physical presence.[3] Instead, they overcome this imbalance by using surprise to their advantage.

Yet, Bradford's approach to preparing his team was very different from Wheaton's. Instead of reviewing every possible scenario and devising a plan against it, Bradford would review only the key parameters of the upcoming mission: What is the mission goal? What is the route to the target? What are the primary threats that the team is likely to face? Bradford and his team would review aerial photos to identify key landmarks, and the team would discuss the ingress and egress strategies. Bradford notes that there was no such thing as an NFL playbook for his SEALs.

On the surface, Wheaton and Bradford appear to have similar jobs: In our conversations with military personnel and the NFL coach,

---

[2] Interview with a retired NFL coach, Santa Monica, Calif., October 30, 2012 (name changed in accordance with research protocol).

[3] Interview with a retired Navy SEAL team leader, Washington, D.C., November 6, 2012 (name changed in accordance with research protocol).

both groups often referred to the other as comparable occupations.[4] However, when it comes to preparing for surprise, the two professions are quite different. The coach devises a contingency plan for everything that could go wrong and instills those plans into his players. The SEAL platoon leader just gives his team a description of the boundary conditions and does not get into detailed "what if" response planning.

These differences provoke some interesting questions about how different professions prepare for and respond to surprise. Why do NFL coaches and Navy SEALs—occupations that are often cited as being analogs of one another—prepare for surprise in such different ways? Why would the SEALs—individuals who risk their lives on every mission—have far fewer "what if" plans than the NFL?

---

[4]   Specifically, the Navy SEAL noted that, as part of his job duties, he had once conducted an analysis that compared U.S. military special forces tactics to those used in the NFL. In addition, the NFL coach noted he had studied military (tactical battle) strategies during his off seasons as a way to identify insightful analogs that might give his team an advantage.

CHAPTER TWO

Why Study Surprise?

Surprise is universal. Virtually all professionals must plan for and deal with unexpected events as part of their daily practice. This makes "occupational" surprise an attractive research topic since the lessons can apply across a range of professions.

Our initial interest in surprise was motivated by work that RAND conducted for the National Reconnaissance Office (NRO). The NRO—indeed, the entire U.S. Intelligence Community—faces an operational environment that is faster paced, more uncertain, and filled with more variables than it was even ten years ago. One of the biggest challenges facing the IC today is that they must confront unknown threats that continue to emerge from unexpected directions. This represents a dramatic contrast to the environment that the IC faced during the Cold War, when the challenges were (relatively speaking) better understood and the circumstances less dynamic. To address these challenges, the NRO asked RAND to identify factors that could help make organizations more agile and responsive.

As part of that larger research effort, RAND proposed a small research project for the NRO Advanced Systems & Technology Directorate (AS&T): What could we learn through conducting an examination of how people in other occupations prepare for and respond to unexpected events? For example, are there practices that medical practitioners, military personnel, or foreign service workers employ that could teach AS&T something about how to better prepare for unexpected events?

After developing this idea further in collaboration with AS&T, we identified two key questions that we sought to answer through this research: Can we become more adept at planning for an uncertain future by studying surprise? What can AS&T learn from studying how different occupations respond to surprise? This report describes the learning exercise that we undertook to address those questions in order to identify recommendations for AS&T.

This report therefore represents our investigation into what diverse professionals believe creates surprise, how they respond to it, and measures they have taken to mitigate its effects. We begin by describing our research objectives and initial hypotheses, including a system to classify professions by the types of surprises they typically encounter. Next, we define our research approach and methods, and then discuss our findings. In presenting those findings, we include anecdotes from actual practitioners to help place the lessons in a real-world context. Our concluding sections offer suggestions on how to both mitigate against the negative effects of surprise and take advantage of the positive opportunities that surprises offer.

CHAPTER THREE

Research Objective, Definitions, and Initial Conceptual Models

The comparison between the football coach and the Navy SEAL suggests how people working in these two occupations adopt divergent approaches toward handling surprise. The objective of our research was to identify how a broad spectrum of professions prepares for and responds to surprise. We sought to identify not only common, effective strategies that those professions used when responding to unexpected events, but also how and why their response strategies differed. This was in the context of our overall research objective, which was to identify practices that may be helpful to professionals in the U.S. Intelligence Community who are regularly faced with unexpected situations.

Our first task was to adopt a working definition of what constitutes surprise. We found a useful starting place in Weick and Sutcliffe's *Managing the Unexpected: Resilience Performance in an Age of Uncertainty* (2007), where the authors identify three types of unexpected events: those that are expected to happen but do not occur, those that are not expected to happen but do occur, and those that were simply not foreseen. The first two types describe events that are imaginable ahead of time; for example, onside kicks in the case of the NFL, or an enemy ambush for the Navy SEAL. Although they are conceivable ahead of time, events of this type are still surprising because they occur infrequently enough that they cannot be easily anticipated. The third type of surprise is sometimes referred to as the "unknown unknown" (UU), and it can represent the most troubling scenario because it can be both unforeseen and unrecognized. For now, we will defer further discussion on distinguishing between different types of surprise, and focus instead on developing a general definition of surprise.

For the purpose of our research, we defined *surprises* as those events that, while the possibility of their occurrence might be known or foreseeable in advance, occur infrequently and with sufficiently low predictability that the timing and circumstances of when and how they arise cannot be anticipated. Onside kicks and enemy ambushes can be imagined ahead of time, but given that occurrences are infrequent, it can be difficult to foresee their circumstances or timing.

The next step in addressing our research goal was to compile an *ad hoc* list of those professions that we assumed must deal with surprise on a regular basis. Throughout this report, we will refer to such professionals as *surprise practitioners;* they pursue careers from corporate executive to emergency room physician to SWAT team commander.[1] We define these individuals as people who encounter surprise or unexpected events during their professional activities. The final version of this list became Table 3.1

To begin our list, we started in what seemed the most natural place: thinking about individuals working in environments where the stakes are high and the pace is fast. Trauma surgeons, emergency room

Table 3.1
Categories of Occupations and Example Professions

High-Stakes, Fast-Paced	Moderate-Stakes, Fast-Paced	Longer-Term Decisionmaking
Trauma surgeons	Improv actors	Diplomats
Emergency room physicians	Taxi drivers	Foreign service officers
Firefighters	Flight attendants	Military general officers
Combat pilots	Photojournalists	Space mission commanders
Arctic fishermen	Public relations officers	Civil engineers
Military special forces	Stock traders	Trial attorneys
Extreme skiers	Professional coaches	Politicians
Hostage negotiators	Chefs	C-level executives
SWAT team commanders		

---

[1]   We use the phrase *surprise practitioners* to describe individuals who are actively engaged in the practice of confronting and responding to surprises as part of their job duties.

physicians, firefighters, combat pilots, Arctic fishermen, military Special Forces operators, extreme sports aficionados, hostage negotiators, and Special Weapons and Tactics (SWAT) team commanders are all good examples of high-stakes professions where people's lives are often also on the line.

In addition to this group, we thought about practitioners who must respond to surprises quickly but do not necessarily face life-or-death scenarios so regularly. For this set, we listed occupations such as professional improvisational actors, taxi drivers, flight attendants, photojournalists, public relations officers, stock traders, coaches in professional sporting leagues, and chefs. All of these individuals need to respond quickly when they encounter the unexpected, but the implications of their decisions are usually somewhat less dire than with the previous group.

The final group we considered included professions that may be less-obvious choices. Although the surprises that this final group encounters may look very different from those facing first responders like firefighters or emergency medical technicians, it is still true that diplomats, military general officers, space mission commanders, civil engineers, trial attorneys, politicians, and chief executive officers (CEOs) all routinely confront their own types of unexpected events. This class of professions is typically associated with longer-term decisionmaking.

As a next step, we sought a way to classify and categorize their surprise "environment." In other words, to examine the spectrum of surprise practitioners, we first needed to define the spectrum itself. At the most basic level, preparing for and responding to surprises is about effective decisionmaking. Therefore, our initial approach was to begin by reviewing the pertinent decision science literature as it relates to unexpected events.

We began with a number of popular works that address various aspects of the surprise problem. As mentioned above, Weick and Sutcliffe's *Managing the Unexpected* (2007) presents a set of rules that "high reliability organizations" (HROs) should follow in order to effectively mitigate the negative effects associated with unexpected events.[2] The rules that the authors identify are based on solid empirical evidence, but we were more interested in the individual than the behavior of the overall enterprise. Bazerman and Watkins' *Predictable Surprises: The Disasters You Should Have Seen Coming, And How to Prevent Them* (2008) focuses on the nature of the surprise itself and they outline a set of characteristics useful for identifying "predictable surprises" before they cascade into more damaging effects. In *Thinking in Time*, Neustadt and May (1986) focus on the utility of using historical analogies to inform present-day decisionmaking. McCall, Lombardo, and Morrison's *Lessons of Experience: How Successful Executives Develop on the Job* (1988) discusses how important experience is for effectively responding to unexpected events.

As we would later confirm, all of the components highlighted in these works—strategies for developing effective response techniques, methods for identifying surprise indicators, developing personal and institutional experience, and leveraging historical analogies—are important elements of an effective preparation and response plan. However, as the starting point of our own research, we needed to understand the theories of how professionals conceptualize surprise when confronting key decision points. This required a relevant model to use as a starting point from which we could develop testable hypotheses to probe through our discussions with expert practitioners.

We found such a model in Gary Klein's *Sources of Power: How People Make Decisions* (1998). Klein's observations and conclusions are not based on controlled laboratory experiments but on careful observation of professionals operating in their natural environment. Klein refers to his approach as operating in "naturalistic decisionmaking settings," by which he means research done "outside the laboratory set-

---

[2] The term *high-reliability organizations* is used by Sutcliffe and Weick to describe organizations that have "no choice but to function reliably. If reliability is compromised, severe harm results" (Weick and Sutcliffe, 2007). Specific examples of HROs include nuclear power plants, air traffic control systems, and hostage negotiation teams.

ting by studying realistic tasks and experienced people working under typical conditions."

Through years of field observations watching firefighters, aircraft carrier operations, and intensive care units, Klein has refined what he calls the "recognition-primed decision model" (RPD), which provides a notional framework for how high-stakes decisions are made (Klein, 1998, p. 7).[3] As Klein notes in his exposition of the model, it fuses two processes: how decisionmakers use prior experience to recognize a situation, and how decisionmakers decide upon an appropriate course of action (Klein, 1998, p. 24). A basic schematic of Klein's RPD model is shown in Figure 3.1.

The model offers three variants: one for dealing with nominal (familiar) events; one for operating when the *cause* of the problem is not

Figure 3.1
Klein's Recognition-Primed Decision Model

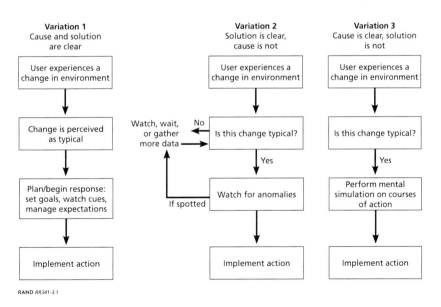

RAND RR341-3.1

---

3   Klein implicitly defines "high stakes" as decisions where the loss of either lives or significant resources is at stake (Klein, 1998, p. 4).

immediately clear; and one for when the proper *action* is not immediately clear. We outline each of these variants below.

The first variant of the RPD model is designed to reflect the nominal process that takes place when most experienced decisionmakers observe a change in their environment: They recognize the change as something they have seen before and they proceed using a previously prescribed course of action. In the most common scenario, practitioners experience a change in their environment but quickly recognize it as a typical situation and proceed with a response plan. As the action is being implemented, the practitioner (instinctively) identifies mental milestones/goals for how their reaction should unfold and therefore also knows what cues will signal that the scenario is not proceeding as expected. According to Klein's concept, this variant of the RPD model describes the firefighter who claims (to Klein) that he never makes decisions, he just acts based on what he observes (Klein, 1998).

But how does the decisionmaking model change when the situation strays from nominal? The second variant of the RPD model applies when the practitioner experiences a situation change, but cannot immediately identify that situation as something familiar. When that happens, the practitioner will diagnose the problem by matching observed features with situations that they have observed in the past. If this is not immediately successful, the practitioner continues to observe the scenario and collect more data. Once the scene is recognized, the practitioner implements the prescribed course of action, being careful to observe for anomalous developments that might indicate the scenario has been misdiagnosed.

The third RPD variant applies when the practitioner can identify the problem but does not have a prescribed solution at hand. Klein suggests that the decisionmaker finds the optimal solution by using mental simulation to evaluate each potential response in order to identify the best option. Once the optimal solution is identified, the decisionmaker can implement that as the proper course of action.

An easy way to distinguish between the three RPD variants is as follows: the first variant is for executing prescribed responses to easily identified problems; the second is for when the problem cannot be immediately identified; the third is when an effective solution cannot be immediately prescribed (Klein, 1998, p. 26).

Klein's model provides an initial framework that describes how professionals make decisions in uncertain environments. The model suggests three key aspects regarding how people respond to surprise:

- Whether conscious or subconscious, decisionmakers rely on a notional decision loop to evaluate and make decisions.
- Decisionmakers will use different mental mechanisms to respond, depending on whether the surprise is immediately recognized.
- When confronted with a situation for which they lack a prescribed solution, decisionmakers use mental simulation to test out potential responses before deciding on a course of action.

Klein's model therefore provided us with three aspects that we sought to consider when developing our hypotheses. (We outline our hypotheses in Chapter Four.)

In addition to the ideas noted above, we were also interested in probing deeper into the nature of the surprise, so we drew inspiration from nine factors that Klein uses to define a naturalistic decision-making setting (2008). These factors are: experienced decisionmakers, high-stakes scenarios, dynamic conditions, inadequate information, time pressure, ill-defined goals, poorly defined procedures, team coordination, and cue learning. Since our research objective required distinguishing between various surprise operating environments, we focused on three key factors of naturalistic decisionmaking settings: time pressure, inadequate information, and dynamic conditions. Those three factors appeared to us to be the ones most likely to influence the approach that experienced professionals use when responding to unexpected events.

For example, our intuition suggested that there should be easily distinguished differences between the jobs of a heart surgeon and a CEO. When in surgery, the thoracic surgeon works in a prescribed environment—the operating room—but is faced with constant decisionmaking every few seconds. The CEO, by contrast, works in a more flexible environment, interacting with a wide group of people in several different settings—such as the board room, his office, via telephone, or in meetings—but is usually not faced with the same intense, life-and-death decisions that the heart surgeon confronts.

Through a process described in detail in the following paragraphs, we refined these factors into a two-dimensional classifying framework, or "surprise space," categorized by *typical response time* and *level of environmental chaos* (which combines the concept of a dynamic environment with one of inadequate information).

Following Klein, we hypothesized that response time was a key distinguishing feature between response strategies. When surprised, some practitioners need to react quickly, while others are usually able to prepare a more deliberate response. One way we thought about this early on was to ask the following question: "Does the profession generally have a 'pause button' when an unexpected event occurs?" Based on this insight we quantized *typical response time* into four discrete points that describe how much time the practitioner generally has to assess and react to a surprise while in that occupation's most common operating mode. Our response time clusters ranged from mere seconds to "days and weeks." An improvisational theater performer, for example, has only seconds to react: While on stage, an "improv" actor faces constant surprises and must respond immediately in order to maintain the flow of the performance. At the other extreme is the CEO, who often (although not always) has the luxury reacting to surprise in time frames that range from days to weeks.

It is important to note that the time involved does not indicate anything about the gravity of the surprise: Although some occupations must respond more quickly than others, this does not necessarily imply that the decisions facing those people carry more or fewer consequences than decisions made in occupations falling elsewhere on the response time line. Response time merely classifies how long practitioners typically have to identify, analyze, and react to surprises once they occur.

The second distinguishing feature that we identified for the professions shown in Table 3.1 is the complexity of their work environment. We recognized that some occupations function in highly chaotic environments with many potential events and distractions, and where several factors may combine to complicate circumstances when a surprise occurs. Other professions work in more sterile environments, where the setting is carefully controlled in order to minimize the role that it plays in creating or complicating surprises. This combines Klein's concepts of a dynamic environment with one of incomplete information.[4]

We define *chaos* as a subjective measure of the frequency, diversity, and predictable orderliness of events (Mitchell, 2009). This definition followed from the recognition that some professions work in more controlled environments than others, and we hypothesized that this would be an important factor when considering how professions approach and respond to surprise. It is worth noting that our definition of chaos differs somewhat from that used in *chaos theory*, wherein chaos refers to dynamic (evolving) systems that are so sensitive to initial changes that it is impossible to predict later events. Our definition incorporates that inability to predict or control events, but also includes a measure of how frequently those events occur, and how disorderly is the resulting environment.

To give an example of different levels of chaos in the work environment, consider the two professions mentioned in the introduction. An NFL coach (or any professional sports coach) works on a defined playing field, with specific rules governing the interactions that take place in that environment. Some football stadiums even have retractable roofs and climate control, further reducing the number of outside factors that can affect gameplay. In addition, the total universe of possible events is relatively sparse, and they tend to unfold individually, one play at a time. By contrast, during an operational mission, a Navy SEAL may encounter surprise and uncertainty from weather, terrain, equipment, colleagues, civilians, adversaries, and even domesticated animals. Thus, the SEAL faces a highly chaotic environment, with many possible events, often occurring simultaneously, and with little hope of controlling or reducing most of the factors that might generate surprise during a mission.

---

[4] Initially, we tried classifying professions simply by the complexity of their work environment (number of possible events) and later by the entropy of the environment (level of orderliness), but eventually settled on the concept of chaos, which combines both ideas.

Distinguishing the operating environment or *surprise space* for various professions using time and level of chaos is useful for several reasons. First, we will show in Chapter Four that they provide a way to categorize the professions and draw distinctions between their operating environments. Second, when populated with actual professions, they allowed us to generate an initial set of hypotheses about how those professions might prepare for and react to surprise, depending on their operating environment. Third, they inspired additional occupations for the list, based on thinking about who needs to operate in each specific surprise environment. Finally, by defining the boundaries of the surprise space, it became possible to select professions to investigate that spanned the entire spectrum outlined by our framework.

The model that we describe so far outlines a framework to both categorize unexpected events and understand how professionals respond to them. We will complete our initial model by adding a final component inspired by the risk-management literature. We include this final component because it helped guide our thinking as we developed the hypotheses discussed in the next chapter.

The first component of the model is a surprise response loop, which served as a universally applicable framework when handling unexpected events. Here, we have summarized Klein's RPD model

Figure 3.2
Simplified Loop for Responding to Surprises

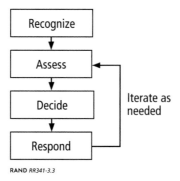

RAND *RR341-3.3*

into a simplified version containing four steps, and the result is displayed in Figure 3.2 (Klein, 1998, p, 27).

The first step in the response loop is to recognize that a surprise is occurring. This led us to the realization that different practitioners probably employ various surprise scanning and recognition strategies, which we would need to explore during our investigation. The second step in the loop is to assess the characteristics and potential consequences of the surprise. Thus, we planned to ask practitioners about their own assessment techniques, including the advantages and limitations of those techniques. The third and fourth steps in the loop are to decide on and implement a response. Different approaches that we thought might be used include selecting from a palate of preplanned response options, following a circumstance-driven protocol, or relying on creativity and ingenuity.

The final component (Figure 3.3) shows that the response strategy will likely depend on when the surprise is discovered and the practitioner takes action to respond. This concept is similar to ideas discussed in the risk-management literature; specifically, that the risk of an event's consequences must be weighed against the cost of preventative measures (Fischhoff et al., 1981).[5]

We recognized that consequences could manifest themselves in different ways: impacts on practitioners' capabilities and/or resources;

Figure 3.3
Response Depends on *When* the Practitioner Responds

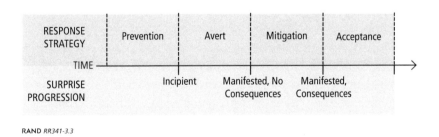

---

[5] For the purpose of this research, we used Willis' definition of risk, which (paraphrased) is the threat of an unwanted—or cascading—aftereffect (Willis et al., 2005).

impacts on mission outcomes; and consequences that might initiate an event cascade. An impact on capabilities or resources is one that might degrade practitioners' ability to carry out their objective without necessarily affecting the eventual outcome; for example, a surprise might force them to expend time and attention dealing with secondary issues such as a wounded soldier, a patient's bleeding artery, or an ejected player. In contrast, other surprises might directly or indirectly affect the actual outcome—for example, by causing the practitioner to lose the battle, the patient, or the game. Finally, another consequence of a surprise might be to initiate a cascading chain of events that must all be addressed in turn.

To probe these ideas in more detail, we developed the framework shown in Figure 3.3. This timeline notes that a surprise often unfolds in stages; as it does, more and more consequences will accrue. We designed this framework as a way to classify the strategies by what stage of the unfolding surprise they addressed. For example, we hypothesized that practitioners could approach surprise at different stages: They could prevent surprises from occurring, work to avert any early consequences, mitigate surprise consequences once they do occur, or let the surprise unfold and simply accept (and deal with) the consequences. We divided these strategies up to help facilitate our interviews with the practitioners, with the hope that it would help us to identify common patterns between different professions. The following four response strategies are described below:

- We define *prevention* as actions taken in advance that are designed to reduce the chances a surprise will occur. There are several examples of prevention, including checklists to avoid surprises that arise from errors of omission, and operating guidelines or rules to prevent surprises that arise from errors of commission. These mechanisms are only useful to the extent that prevention will be effective: Many surprises may be too difficult to predict or control in advance.
- *Averting consequences* requires responding to a surprise after it occurs but before any consequences have accrued. This approach will only work if a practitioner can recognize early that a surprise

is unfolding and stop it before the effects proliferate. We believed that some relevant approaches might include continuously scanning for threats as a default activity or using other forms of trained pattern recognition. Even so, it might not be possible to detect many surprises at this initial stage, or to take effective action so early. Thus, mitigating the consequences of a surprise is often necessary.

- *Mitigation* refers to a class of actions designed to lessen the pain or reduce the severity of an outcome (Baiocchi, 2010). Mitigation does not address the root cause, but instead works to effectively treat the symptoms. Some specific mitigation approaches might include using special tools to solve the problem (either physical or mental), employing teamwork, relying on redundant systems, or simply devoting extra resources (time, money, or manpower) toward the expected consequences.
- We also considered the idea of *acceptance*: In some cases, expending effort to cope with a surprise might be a worse or more costly approach than just accepting the consequences and moving on. In that case, practitioners would need strategies to help them quickly recognize the need to cut their losses.

In the next chapter, we will use all of these mental tools that we developed in this chapter to generate our research hypotheses.

CHAPTER FOUR

Research Hypotheses

After establishing the two key axes for our surprise space and identifying candidate professions, we next began to generate hypotheses about how practitioners in different parts of the surprise space might handle surprises. Figure 4.1 shows the axes populated with a sample set of professions.[1] Our goal when populating the array was to find one or two occupations for each intersection of X and Y axes. We began with the list shown in Table 3.1 and populated the surprise space with a subset of these professions. Examining the results allowed us to start generating hypotheses about how different professions might respond to surprise.

In Figure 4.1, each occupation's preliminary placement on the response-time axis reflected our initial belief regarding the profession's *usual* operating mode, and not necessarily their only response time frame. For example, while a lieutenant general in the U.S. Air Force may have to respond within minutes or even seconds to some surprises, we believed that an Air Force general usually has a few hours to respond under most scenarios. The second point worth noting is that our assumptions were necessarily based on an outsider's view of how each profession operated. As we will describe in the next section, we later conducted expert discussions to confirm that we had all the professions positioned in the correct location. Not all of our assumptions turned out to be correct, with the result that a few professions needed to be relocated within the surprise space. The axes shown in Figure 4.1 represent our final version of the

---

[1] We will provide more details about our research method, including why we chose the professions that we did, in Chapter Five.

Figure 4.1
Framework for Classifying Professions by Typical Response Time and Level of Chaos in the Work Environment

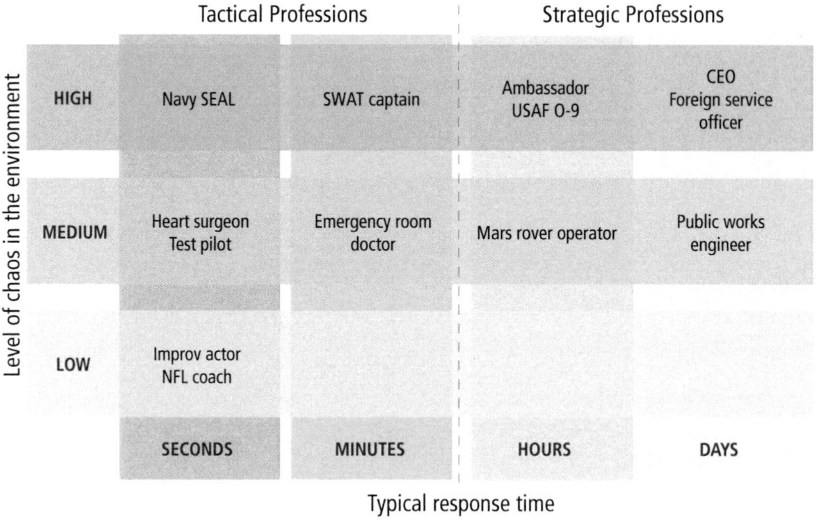

		Tactical Professions		Strategic Professions	
					CEO
HIGH		Navy SEAL	SWAT captain	Ambassador USAF O-9	Foreign service officer
MEDIUM		Heart surgeon Test pilot	Emergency room doctor	Mars rover operator	Public works engineer
LOW		Improv actor NFL coach			
		SECONDS	**MINUTES**	**HOURS**	**DAYS**

Level of chaos in the environment

Typical response time

RAND RR341-4.1

figure based on both our initial assumptions and the results from the expert discussions.

Most of the spots on Figure 4.1 are populated with at least one profession, but we chose not to populate the lower right portion of the space for two reasons. First, we had a hard time identifying occupations that could occupy these slots. Second, even if we could identify professions that met the criteria, we hypothesized that the lessons those occupations might yield were unlikely to be broadly useful: Practitioners who work in low-chaos environments and have days or weeks to respond when surprises do occur are unlikely to have many lessons to offer. Our overall objective was to identify ways that people and organizations could become more flexible, and we believe there is less to be learned about flexibility from occupations that operate in low-chaos environments with response times on the order of days or weeks.

Before beginning our conversations with surprise practitioners, we needed specific, testable hypotheses about how different professions handle surprise. As we described in the previous section, we started with Klein's RPD model as a starting point, and we developed the framework shown in Figure 3.2 in order to further probe the factors associated with response time and environmental chaos. From these ideas, we developed five hypotheses:

Hypothesis 1: Response Time Affects How Practitioners Prepare for and Respond to Surprises

Our first hypothesis came from an observation that the professions in Figure 4.1 can be split into two groups, left and right, based on their available response time once a surprise occurs. Those professions on the left side of the figure often have to respond within seconds or minutes, leaving them little time to develop a comprehensive response plan. Responses must be planned in advance or improvised on the spot. We therefore referred to these occupations as the *tactical professions*, using the military's connotation of the word tactical. In military usage, a tactical operation is one that requires or involves near-term support actions (within a short time frame). While incidental to this hypothesis, one observation about most of the tactical professions is that they are skilled in touch-labor: they work with their hands.[2] This observation is likely due to the fact that all of these professionals need to get things done *quickly*, and personally interacting with their environment—typically with one's hands—is the best way to be most responsive.

In contrast, professions on the right-hand side of the surprise space—which we referred to as the *strategic professions*—have more time to plan and organize their response following a surprise.[3] Essentially, all of these professions also fit within a category that most people

---

[2] There are some exceptions, such as improv actors, and public relations spokespeople. We did explore differences between the touch and knowledge tactical professions, but only to a limited degree.

[3] In using the terms *strategic* and *tactical* occupations, we recognize that those individuals working in more tactical occupations certainly engage in long-term (strategic) planning, and vice versa for strategic professions. We use the terms *strategic* and *tactical* to indicate the professions' most common operating modes when responding to unexpected events.

would recognize as knowledge workers: these occupations provide value through their intellectual capital and professional relationships.[4]

This distinction between the two groups motivated our first hypothesis: Does the amount of response time affect the way that practitioners prepare for and respond to surprise? Does a CEO do the same things as a heart surgeon when encountering surprise, or do they use fundamentally different approaches? We suspected, for example, that tactical professions would rely more on preplanned protocols and doctrine, while the strategic professions would have more flexibility. The reason behind this thinking is suggested by Klein's model: Decision-makers who are short on time generally prefer to pursue a prepackaged, proven response.

Hypothesis 2: The Level of Environmental Chaos Affects How Professionals Prepare for and Respond to Surprise

Our second hypothesis was motivated by the observation that the surprise space depicted in Figure 4.1 can be divided from top to bottom based on the level of environmental chaos. The professions at the top of the space all face high levels of chaos, with many possible surprise scenarios and a limited ability to predict or influence their occurrence. In a high-chaos environment, it is likely more difficult to craft a specific response for each possible surprise or to take preventive action that keeps surprises from occurring. It might also be more difficult to distinguish an incipient surprise from the many other distracting but unimportant events that occur in such a noisy environment.

These distinctions between the two environments evoked our second hypothesis, which gave rise to the following questions: Does the level of chaos in the environment drive the way these two groups

---

[4]   By associating the term "knowledge workers" with the more strategically oriented professions, we inadvertently suggest that the tactical professions are not valued for their own knowledge capital. This is certainly not our intent. We chose to use the term "knowledge worker" because it is a phrase that is already part of the vernacular, and the colloquial meaning is in convenient alignment with our "strategic professions."

handle surprise? Does the Navy SEAL use the same planning and response techniques as an emergency room doctor or an NFL coach?

Hypothesis 3: The Surprise Type Dictates the Reaction and Response Path

We had three additional hypotheses that applied more generally across all of the professions. The first had to do with the *type* of surprise, and is based on Klein's observation that the response will depend on whether the surprise is recognized or not. As we mentioned earlier, Weick and Sutcliffe (2007) identify three different types of surprises: expected that do not happen, unexpected that do happen, and what the authors refer to as "unthought of" surprises.

For our purposes, we simplified these three instances into two categories: *known unknowns* (KUs) and *unknown unknowns* (UUs). This concept owes its notoriety to a famous statement by then–Secretary of Defense Donald Rumsfeld. While making the case for invading Iraq despite the incomplete evidence linking that country to terrorists or weapons of mass destruction, he said:

> There are known knowns; there are things we know we know.

> We also know there are known unknowns; that is to say, we know there are some things we do not know.

> But there are also unknown unknowns—the ones we don't know we don't know.[5]

In fact, the concept of UUs was in common use by the aerospace community since at least the 1960s, and in the military context since at least the 1970s (Myers, 1969, p. 76). For the purpose of our conceptual

---

[5]   Donald Rumsfeld, speaking at a U.S. Department of Defense press conference on February 12, 2002; reprinted as a poem in Seely (2003, p. 2).

model, we defined KUs as surprises that either have already happened at least once before or can be foreseen fairly easily as possible sometime in the future. UUs, by contrast, are those surprise events that are so unlikely or so far outside theory and experience that they are not considered part of the universe of events worth considering until they actually occur. Thus, by definition, they are always a surprise when they occur. These are the so-called "black swan" events studied by Nassim Taleb (2007).

An excellent example of a KU surprise was suggested to us by a retired Air Force general officer, who noted that following the first Gulf War, then–Iraqi President Saddam Hussein had a fairly consistent habit of launching missile strikes against enemy targets around the start of Muslim holidays. Those in the American armed forces did not know where the attack was going to occur, but they knew from experience that an attack was a possibility. Thus, the missile attacks were a KU: Air Force generals recognized that attacks were likely, but the lack of knowledge regarding locations and targets still meant the attacks were a surprise.[6]

A senior diplomat noted that the 1986 Chernobyl disaster was a good example of a UU.[7] The disaster itself was entirely unexpected and presented a variety of diplomatic challenges that could not have been foreseen before the event occurred. For example, the large scale of the disaster required the coordination of many types of technical personnel (such as nuclear physicists) alongside politicians from different countries, which at the time was an unprecedented necessity.

This Chernobyl example helps to clarify an important point: A UU need not be considered an impossible event—certainly, a nuclear plant meltdown was always possible, but was thought so unlikely to ever affect the Foreign Service that they never considered such an event or its potential ramifications. As Taleb (2007) has expounded at length, most black swan events occur as UUs for this very reason: The probability that they might occur was miscalculated as being much

---

[6]   Interview with a retired U.S. Air Force general officer, Santa Monica, Calif., November 9, 2012 (name withheld in accordance with research protocol).

[7]   Interview with a former U.S. ambassador, Washington D.C., November 7, 2012 (name withheld in accordance with research protocol).

lower than the actual risk. For another example of such UUs, consider the recent frequency of so-called "once in a century" hurricanes, super storms, and other extreme weather events.

Since surprise practitioners will never make specific advanced preparations for a UU, and since such events are also likely to present novel challenges, we suspected that different response strategies might come into play when they occurred. Thus, an additional research goal became investigating how the type of surprise affected surprise practitioners' response. Does the response strategy for a KU differ from that for a UU?

Hypothesis 4: Strategies for Addressing Positive Surprises Differ from Those for Negative Ones

Our fourth hypothesis arose after we recognized an unconscious assumption: We had been automatically assuming that all surprises have negative implications. Could some surprises have positive implications? The answer was obvious—of course they can.[8]

Our fourth hypothesis is therefore related to the nature of the surprise: Are the response strategies different for positive versus negative surprises? Is it possible that the strategies used by surprise practitioners who must constantly guard against negative surprises—the SWAT team commanders or Navy SEALs, for example—prevent them from perceiving or taking advantage of positive surprises when they occur?

Hypothesis 5: Some Fundamental Preparations and Responses Are Common Across Professions

Finally, we returned to our original research goal: searching out techniques or lessons for addressing the effects caused by surprise that are common across all of the professions, regardless of available response

---

[8]   One of the best examples of using surprise (from an opponent) to an advantage came from the NFL coach. He noted that surprises on the football field are often good opportunities for a counterattack because they are usually risky, less-rehearsed scenarios that are easier to leverage if properly prepared to do so (Interview, October 30, 2012).

time or level of environmental chaos. Are there response techniques or mental tools that all of the professions rely on? Klein's RPD model is certainly universal, which suggests that we would find common techniques applicable across multiple professions.

To summarize, after considering the implications of our initial conceptual model, the goal of our research was to address the following questions:

- What strategies are common across all of the professions? Are there techniques and tools that everyone uses, regardless of their environment or required reaction time?
- Does the level of environmental chaos determine how various professions respond to surprise?
- Do the tactical professions take a uniformly different approach to responding to surprise than the strategic occupations?
- Does the type of surprise matter? Do professionals respond differently to KUs versus UUs?
- Is the appropriate response for surprises with positive implications different from that for negative surprises? Does routinely confronting negative surprises interfere with capitalizing on positive surprises when they occur?

As we will show, our conversations with experienced surprise practitioners would alter or disprove several of our initial beliefs. However, this considerable preparatory effort gave us both a starting place for those conversations and a mental map of where we needed to direct our questions. This preparation made the subsequent conversations more productive, and it helped us to recognize key information and insights when they arose. As Louis Pasteur observed in 1854, "in the field of observation, chance only favors the prepared mind" (Pasteur, 1939, p. 131).

CHAPTER FIVE

Research Method

Our overall goal was to better understand how professionals deal with surprise, seeking to uncover lessons that would be generally applicable to other surprise practitioners. As we have already described, we began by generating the list of professions shown in Table 3.1. Next we developed a two-dimensional "surprise space," shown in Figure 3.1, that builds on features noted in Klein's decisionmaking model. This surprise space serves as a framework for organizing different professions according to the chaos of their operating environment and the amount of time available to respond to surprises.

The next step was to populate the array with examples of professions chosen from the original list. Our aim was to span the spectrum of surprise environments by selecting an occupation for most of the positions within the surprise space. We made these selections based on several inclusion criteria. The first factor was entirely pragmatic: With limited time and resources, we wanted to select professions for which we were confident we could readily recruit and speak with an experienced practitioner. Second, we felt that examining a variety of professions created an asset that helped meet our research objective. By interviewing a diverse set of practitioners (instead of just health care providers, for example), we hoped to access a wider range of backgrounds and perspectives. Indeed, as we will describe, this did prove valuable since we heard similar themes emerge from seemingly different perspectives, which helped reinforce the notion that the response strategies we were hearing were robust and applied across multiple professions.

In addition to these primary criteria, we also required that our participating practitioners had

- at least ten years of post-training professional experience
- achieved a high supervisory or equivalent level of responsibility
- otherwise distinguished themselves (through commendations, awards, or peer recognition) as a superior performer in their field.

We imposed these additional criteria because we assumed that speaking with experienced and successful individuals would be the most efficient way to learn about effective best practices.

We were fortunate in that everyone that we attempted to speak with agreed to participate in the project. The list of interviewees included 13 occupations: CEO, retired U.S. ambassador, test pilot, foreign service officer, cardiothoracic surgeon, recently retired Navy SEAL, recently retired NFL coach, professional improv actor, public works/civil engineer, space mission planner/operator, recently retired Air Force general officer, SWAT team commander, and emergency room physician.[1]

Our intent with all of the interviews was to achieve three goals. The first was to assess that we had accurately positioned the professions within our surprise space in Figure 4.1 in Chapter Four. To do this, part of our conversation with each representative sought to get a sense of how quickly they had to react when responding to surprise. We also

---

[1] Interviews with: NFL coach, October 30, 2012; Navy SEAL team leader, November 6, 2012; retired U.S. Air Force general officer, November 9, 2012; U.S. ambassador, November 7, 2012; retired combat pilot and current test pilot, Mojave, Calif., October 24, 2012; CEO of a firm with 1,200 worldwide employees, Arlington, Va., November 8, 2012; small-business CEO and active management consultant, Arlington, Va., November 7, 2012; university hospital chief of cardiothoracic surgery, Santa Monica, Calif., October 25, 2012; senior SWAT team captain, Santa Monica, Calif., November 2, 2012; two Mars Rover personnel at the Jet Propulsion Laboratories (JPL), Pasadena, Calif., November 15, 2012; a major projects public works engineer, Santa Monica, Calif., October 30, 2012; veteran academic emergency department physician, Santa Monica, Calif., October 22, 2012; prominent professional improvisational theater instructor and performer, Santa Monica, Calif., November 11, 2012; former U.S. foreign service officer, Santa Monica, Calif., November 15, 2012 (names withheld in accordance with research protocol).

asked them questions about their operating environment to make sure that our estimate about the level of chaos was accurate.

The second goal was to learn more about the techniques and tools each used when responding to surprise. To probe these topics, we asked the practitioners to tell us about how they typically responded to surprise and what (if any) professional or organizational protocols they relied on when responding. Questions were based on our hypotheses and a list of discussion items, but the conversations were allowed to progress organically.

The final goal was to obtain anecdotes that could be used to support and illustrate our findings. Participants offered a surprisingly rich and varied set of such stories, many of which we share in the following sections.

We conducted semistructured interviews with practitioners from each profession to achieve the three goals mentioned above. Before beginning the interview process, we developed a protocol that outlined the key topics we hoped to discuss in every conversation. Specifically, we focused on addressing the following issues:

- What is the level of chaos and usual available response time in the typical operating environment?
- What are some other parameters and constraints of the typical operating environment?
- What are their profession's criteria for operational success or failure?
- What role does surprise play in their operating environment?
- What does the response process look like when surprises occur?
- What resources, tools, and strategies are available for dealing with surprise, and how are they typically applied?
- How much do flexibility and finesse apply when dealing with surprise?
- To what extent are surprises viewed as opportunities rather than obstacles?
- What are the key elements to successfully deal with surprise? What are some examples of when those approaches failed?

- What are some characteristics of a professional in their field that allows the person to best handle surprise?
- Finally, we always gave participants the opportunity to express additional thoughts on topics that had not been covered earlier.

Specific prompts and example questions were available to use as needed, but in general the discussions were allowed to flow naturally without a mandated sequence or structure. We used an open-ended interview process that allowed us to gain nuances unlikely to be provided by a more statistically oriented study. Our conversation with each practitioner lasted between 45 and 90 minutes, with approximately half of them conducted by phone and the other half in person. Two researchers participated in each discussion, with one taking the lead role and the other primarily taking detailed notes.

Everyone that we spoke with was at the top of their profession, generally a senior leader or key actor in organizations that would be instantly recognizable to most people. One reason we chose prominent individuals was because we assumed that their success was due in part to their effectiveness at dealing with unexpected events. We have refrained from disclosing the names of the people we spoke with because part of our research approach was to promise our participants anonymity. We did this to encourage accuracy and objectivity when describing any sensitive aspects of their operating environment, which we deemed more important than borrowing credibility by citing the names of well-known individuals or organizations within a particular career field.

Data from each conversation was analyzed using qualitative methods. Both investigators discussed the content and debriefed each other within 24 hours following each conversation. We compared information provided by each participant against the relevant components of our initial conceptual model, looking for confirmation, disconfirmation, and novel insights or features. We used the information that participants provided about their methods and processes to test our hypotheses.

We also compared their descriptions against those provided by the other participants, looking for subjective similarities and differences in their approaches to surprise. The goal of this exercise was to identify key themes across the different professions. Where differences in approach could be identified, we also attempted to characterize any associated differences in the surprise environment between those professions. These iterative updates to our initial hypotheses, including any tentative conclusions regarding the reasons for differences and similarities in approaches between professions, were then subsequently tested when discussing related topics with other professionals. Following the completion of our discussions with all recruited professionals, the results of this analysis were then organized and grouped by initial hypothesis.

It was not our intent to evaluate our interview data using quantitative or statistical means. For example, we did not set out to make statements like, "75 percent of all CEOs rely on the same method to respond to an unexpected event." Such an approach was not in alignment with our project's goal of simply identifying general trends across the professions. A second reason is that our interview sample of 15 professionals lacked meaningful statistical power.

How did we know that interviewing 15 professionals was sufficient to meet our goal and identify general trends? For guidance on this, we followed a suggestion by Robert S. Weiss in *Learning from Strangers: The Art and Method of Qualitative Interview Studies* (2008): "You stop when you encounter diminishing returns, when the information you obtain is redundant or peripheral." About two-thirds of the way through the interview process, we began to hear familiar narratives over again, a good indication that our small data set was providing reliable data. For example, we repeatedly heard representatives from seemingly different occupations using virtually identical language when describing their response techniques. One of the CEOs we spoke with used exactly the same vocabulary as the Navy SEAL when describing how he reacts to a surprise event.[2] All these examples suggest that we had reached what survey managers call the "saturation point," which is a good indication that the number of interviews was sufficient for meeting our research objective. We hope that the anecdotes that we describe in our findings will similarly convince readers of the genuine similarities between seemingly different occupations.

---

[2] Interview with CEO of firm with 1,200 worldwide employees, November 8, 2012.

CHAPTER SIX

What Strategies Are Common Across Professions?

We begin the discussion of our results by highlighting four strategies that we found common to virtually all practitioners we interviewed. We list them briefly before providing more detail and context on each:

- **Experience is a key element in dealing with surprise.** Nearly everyone we spoke with told us there is no substitute for experience, which is one of the most effective ways to reduce the number and severity of surprise effects. Intuitively, this makes sense: Those practitioners with experience are less likely to be surprised because they have seen and experienced so many scenarios and outcomes throughout their career.
- **Reducing the level of chaos within the operating environment can mitigate the negative effects of surprise.** All interviewees said they take measures to reduce the level of environmental chaos, and thus the likelihood that they will be surprised during day-to-day operations. The specific measures vary depending on the environment, but all practitioners offered evidence that they actively employ measures to reduce environmental chaos.
- **Match the surprise response to the actual need.** Everyone we spoke with noted the importance of keeping one's emotions in check when responding to surprise. They indicated that one key implication following a surprise was the need to initially deploy a measured level of resources to deal with the event, rather than reflexively using all available resources at the first opportunity.

- **Teamwork reduces both the chance of surprise and the severity of a surprise when it occurs.** The value of teams cannot be understated: Practitioners rely on colleagues to plan and prepare for surprises, scan for and report surprises when they occur, and refine and execute responses.

Experience Is Key

The most common phrase we heard from everyone we spoke with was that "there is no substitute for experience." Experience is most effective when dealing with surprise because it reduces the size of the surprise space. Experienced practitioners can recognize many nascent surprises early, before they can cause too many adverse effects. This, in turn, allows practitioners to prevent those surprises or avert significant consequences. For example, a CEO with 20 years of experience described how he is much less likely to be caught offguard than a newly minted graduate with a master's in business administration because his experience makes him better able to accurately predict how events will unfold and take measures to avoid or avert certain outcomes.[1] In addition, when a surprise does occur, the experienced CEO has a larger solution set to draw upon because he will have faced a larger and more varied set of problems.

We heard a similar refrain from the thoracic surgeon.[2] He cited a number of times when something unexpected happened in the operating room and he was able to draw on a previous experience as a way to quickly formulate an effective plan for how he should proceed. He noted that most heart surgeries are fairly straightforward and doctors can just follow a standard procedure, which he felt explained why so many (relatively) mediocre heart surgeons remain successful. Experience only comes into play when something unexpected happens, and

---

[1]   Interview with small-business CEO, November 7, 2012.

[2]   Cardiothoracic surgeons generally operate on organs inside the chest. The surgeon we spoke with specializes in operations to repair faulty hearts, including heart transplants. Interview with chief of thoracic surgery, October 25, 2012.

only then do you need someone who has the confidence and deep knowledge base that comes with so much experience. He went on to note that one of his roles as a teacher was to help surgeons with less experience develop that expertise under controlled conditions.

The test pilot, who had also flown fighters in combat, reported a similar phenomenon. When training test and fighter pilots, he would often see a "surprise" situation developing long before it actually occurred, while the trainee remained oblivious until much later. Within the limits of safety, he would let surprises occur and allow the trainees to work their way through, helping them to develop not only skill in dealing with that situation but also, he believed, the experience to recognize and avoid that surprise in the future.[3]

Together, all of these practitioners had developed their intuition for surprise, which we believe is primarily due to better judgment based on prior experience. This lesson is best captured by an anonymously attributed expression: "Good judgment comes from experience. Experience comes from bad judgment." This ties directly back to Klein's work, which suggested that the easiest type of surprise situation to diagnose and respond to is one that is perceived as "typical."[4] Recognizing a "typical" surprise likewise allows the practitioner to deploy a previously proven response strategy (and also often allow them to deploy their response earlier). Experience is one of the primary ways to build up a practitioner's set of typical scenarios.

Finally, we note something that we heard from many of our participants, phrased along the following lines: "If I'm doing my job right, there shouldn't be any surprises." As we will show in the next section, this statement is most applicable to the tactical professions working in less-chaotic environments but we also heard this response from the CEO and the ambassador. The CEO, for example, noted that it was his primary job to be looking toward the horizon and making correc-

---

[3] Interview with test pilot, October 24, 2012.

[4] In addition to our findings being supported by Klein's work, this perspective is also consistent with reporting from the academic literature that looks at how grand chess masters make decisions. While the exact mechanisms are still being debated, there is a general consensus that a chess master's experience allows for an improved ability to recognize patterns and plan more successful future moves.

tive actions to ensure that the organization would not be forced to face critical surprises, but added that it takes a concerted effort to always be thinking strategically.[5]

We will discuss this concept more when we address how strategists react to surprise.

Reduce the Level of Chaos

The most common behavior we observed across the professions is that all practitioners said they take measures to reduce the level of chaos—the number of unknowns and complicating variables—within their work environment. Chaos is undesirable when dealing with surprise for several reasons: It increases the number of potential surprises; it increases the difficulty in discriminating surprises from unimportant background events; it may magnify the severity of an unexpected event; and chaos may also make it difficult to determine the root cause of a surprise once it has occurred. A main goal is therefore to simplify the problem.

The most straightforward example of this strategy in a high-chaos environment came from the SWAT team commander.[6] When a call to activate the SWAT team arrives, the SWAT captain approaches the situation knowing that he does not have all of the facts. When a police patrol encounters a problem that might require SWAT intervention, they call their sergeant, who calls the watch commander, who calls the metro desk. By the time the SWAT captain is contacted, he is likely getting information about the incident from someone who is two or three degrees removed from the scene. Thus, the SWAT captain recognizes from the start that he does not have a complete picture and that there is likely missing information that would affect his team's appropriate response and could generate unnecessary surprises. He refers to new information that alters his assessment as a "feature change."

---

[5]   Interview with small-business CEO, November 7, 2012; interview with U.S. ambassador, November 7, 2012.

[6]   Interview with SWAT team captain, November 2, 2012.

Therefore, his method in moving forward is to try to fill in as many of the missing pieces of information as possible. For example, if the watch commander is the first person to call him, the captain asks to speak with personnel who are on scene. He asks if animals are involved. He asks his research team to start generating some background on the people involved. Throughout the entire process, the captain asks himself, "What don't I know, and how could this cause a feature change?"

By acknowledging he does not know everything, the SWAT captain is increasing his odds of success. First, his mind-set is designed to make him automatically do "what if" planning: What would happen if a piece of evidence turns out to be true? How would he react then? What could he start doing now to mitigate that effect in the future? Second, this mind-set serves as a reliable method for approaching surprises. By constantly seeking the missing information, the captain is methodically working toward an optimal solution.

Another approach to reducing chaos that we heard repeatedly involved controlling the environment to minimize variation. The heart surgeon, for example, always sets up his operating room the same way, with instruments in the same arrangement and with many of the same staffing choices. He also follows set procedures, seeking to avoid introducing any new variables into the equation.[7] Similarly, the test pilot and Mars rover teams usually only perform one maneuver at a time, so as not to complicate the operational situation.[8]

This insight also ties back Klein's work. By controlling the level of environmental chaos, practitioners simplify two tasks of the RPD model. The first is that they are more likely to identify a surprise situation as a simple match to a typical situation. If it appears unfamiliar at first, there will be fewer features to parse to make a match. The second advantage is that if a situation is truly not typical, limiting the number of variables will make it easier to mentally simulate response scenarios and chose the most viable one.

---

[7] Interview with chief of thoracic surgery, October 25, 2012.

[8] Interview with test pilot, October 24, 2012; interview with Mars Rover personnel, November 15, 2012.

Practically speaking, this suggests that most occupations can benefit from mechanisms that help reduce the level of chaos when operating in a surprise environment. As we will show in the next section, the exact mechanism depends on whether the practitioner works in a tactical profession or a strategic one, so we will reserve more specific recommendations for that discussion.

Provide a Measured Response

When responding to surprise, virtually all the practitioners that we spoke with noted the importance of a measured response. We detected two different but related messages: the first emphasized the importance of keeping emotions under control; the second stressed judicious deployment of material resources.

Both CEOs we spoke with noted the importance of keeping emotions in check and not acting impulsively immediately after the surprise.[9] One of them shared how he has started responding to email surprises in a different way than he used to. Before, he would quickly type out and send his response, which would often end up being too full of emotion and not enough objectivity. Now, he notes that he will still type out the quick response, but he generally saves the message as a draft for at least 24 hours. This allows him to revisit the message before sending it, which lets him confirm that his response is constructively based on objectivity and facts rather than raw emotion. Similarly, when presented with a lawsuit, his first, emotional reaction previously had been to respond aggressively to what he felt was an affront on his honor. More recently, he has learned to objectively assess the most business-appropriate response before acting.[10]

All of the tactical professions also reported the need to control emotion when a surprise occurred. Generally, their complicating emotion was panic, rather than anger. In a tactical profession, a rapid

---

[9]   Interview with small-business CEO, November 7, 2012; interview with CEO of a firm with 1,200 worldwide employees, November 8, 2012.

[10]   Interview with CEO of a firm with 1,200 worldwide employees, November 8, 2012.

response is often essential. Nevertheless, every practitioner we spoke with described how their first action when a potentially serious surprise occurred was to force themselves toward calm. Each profession has a different descriptive term, but the concept is the same: An improv actor thinks "yes, and . . ." Test pilots are trained to "wind the clock," by which they mean take a moment to do (at least figuratively) a simple menial task like winding a mechanical watch. Good surgeons channel their anxiety into productive actions. NFL coaches call an actual "time out." All of these mental maneuvers are designed to forestall a precipitous reaction and buy a few moments to calm down and select the proper response.

Even if panic and overconfidence are not a factor, the instinctive reaction to a surprise is to respond with a maximal deployment of available resources. Several practitioners pointed out why this is not a good idea. For example, the recently retired Air Force general officer was in command of one of the military's major logistics resources on September 11, 2001. After the first attack occurred, he recognized immediately that there would be a need for his organization's resources. He also recognized that the scope and nature of the situation remained unclear, so he initially deployed only a common denominator of resources, or units that would be essential regardless of the specific response.[11]

When we asked him about this, he emphasized that he did not deploy everything he had for two key reasons. First, he wanted to maintain a strategic reserve to deal with possible later contingencies. He also wanted to avoid committing resources to the wrong task or destination before any specific transportation requests arrived at his desk. In this instance, he was able to rely on a premeditated plan: Long before 9/11, he had spent considerable time thinking about which resources would be needed to cover most national emergency scenarios. When 9/11 occurred, he ended up deploying the prescribed measure of resources outlined in his plan.[12]

Similarly, calling in a SWAT team is not a decision senior police leaders take lightly. The SWAT captain we spoke with noted that

---

[11] Interview with U.S. Air Force general officer, November 9, 2012.

[12] Interview with U.S. Air Force general officer, November 9, 2012.

deploying a SWAT team engages a tremendous number of resources: highly trained personnel, canines, specialized equipment, armored vehicles, and air support. Employing those resources is expensive for—not to mention disruptive to—the local community, and this is something our SWAT captain is mindful of whenever he gets the call from personnel on scene. He is also aware that deploying his team can escalate a situation, potentially increasing the likelihood that deadly force will be used by the authorities, which may not always be appropriate to the circumstances.[13]

There are therefore two lessons that trained and experienced surprise practitioners taught us using these anecdotes about providing a measured response. The first is that your initial, instinctive reaction is not always the best one, and the second is that more response is not always a better response.

The Value of Teamwork

Before our interview, our assumptions about a test pilot's occupation were mostly based on the depiction of Chuck Yeager in *The Right Stuff* (Wolfe, 1983): a lone maverick, risking his life to test the unknown limits of a new machine. The truth turned out to be the exact opposite and we had to revise our initial model to account for the role teamwork plays in successfully responding to surprise events.

The test pilot is responsible for executing the mission, and his senses—primarily touch and hearing—are often the first things to detect a problem. However, to mitigate the chances of a life-threatening surprise, the plane is heavily instrumented with sensors designed to detect the most likely failure scenarios. While the pilot is in the air, a team of flight engineers on the ground are constantly monitoring the aircraft for any sign of trouble. Whether the pilot or the ground team is the first to detect something unexpected, there is a good chance one of the engineers will be able to identify the source of the problem using the plane's telemetry. This allows the engineers to

---

[13] Interview with SWAT team captain, November 2, 2012.

inform the pilot of the problem's most likely cause.[14] Thus, the team approach not only reduces the level of chaos in the cockpit but also reduces how many solutions the pilot must consider.

We learned that we had made similarly false assumptions about the role of teamwork for the heart surgeon and CEO. The popular depiction of a highly technical physician suggests a lone doctor, accompanied by an anesthesiologist and perhaps a few nurses. The heart surgeon we spoke with noted that during the most complicated procedures, he often has three distinct teams in the operating room with him: one for anesthesia, a second to run the heart/lung bypass machine, and a third that handles the surgical tools and additional patient support equipment. The surgeon reported that little surprises constantly unfold within these teams during procedures, but that he is often unaware of them because they are addressed by the appropriate team. He noted that a surprise has to be rather serious to rise to his level.[15] Thus, the surgeon relies heavily on his teams to resolve the smaller surprises. In the event that the surprise is serious enough to require the surgeon's attention, he relies on his team to provide additional data and context to help him identify the root cause and help devise a plan to address it. As with the test pilot, teamwork helps reduce the level of chaos in the operating room and simplifies the surgeon's task when resolving more serious surprises.

The CEOs we spoke with provided us with similar narratives. Both individuals noted that they rarely made unilateral decisions. Instead, they relied on management teams consisting of trusted coworkers to provide additional context and perspective.[16]

Based on those descriptions, we believe teamwork serves two key roles. The first is to expand the available cognitive resources. When facing a complex task, especially in the face of time pressure, having the ability to think through and manage multiple elements at once may be beyond any one person's capabilities. A second role, also implied by

---

[14] Interview with combat pilot, October 24, 2012.

[15] Interview with chief of thoracic surgery, October 25, 2012.

[16] Interview with small-business CEO, November 7, 2012.; interview with CEO of a firm with 1,200 worldwide employees, November 8, 2012.

Klein's model, is that teamwork widens the pool of available experience, making it easier to recognize a surprise situation and elect a response.

The natural conclusion from these observations is that teamwork must be a key component of the culture when an organization is trying to mitigate effects caused by surprise. As we will discuss later, strategists rely particularly heavily on a trusted network of "direct reports" (personnel reporting directly to them) to achieve an effective response to surprise.

CHAPTER SEVEN

How Does the Level of Environmental Chaos Affect Practitioners' Responses to Surprises?

Our initial model assumed that the level of environmental chaos was a primary influence on how practitioners prepare for surprise. Our discussions with surprise practitioners supported this hypothesis, but they also revealed some new insights about levels of chaos. We will summarize the two basic concepts that we were able to confirm, along with three unexpected insights:

- **In less chaotic environments, practitioners rely more on specific, preplanned "what if" responses.** Intuitively, this observation makes sense: If the size of the surprise space is small enough that the practitioner can reasonably develop a response plan for every possible scenario, then it makes sense to do so.
- **In more complex environments, practitioners cannot afford to develop "what if" plans for all contingencies, but instead develop general response frameworks useful in a variety of surprise situations.** Preplanning tended to focus on identifying enabling actions, or immediate steps that would preserve their options and facilitate more specific responses that came later. Those practitioners working in the most complex environments—the CEO and the Navy SEAL— also told us that developing more-detailed "what if" response plans, even for KUs, limited their ability to think creatively when a surprise event occurs.[1]

---

[1] Interview with CEO of a firm with 1,200 worldwide employees, November 8, 2012; interview with Navy SEAL team leader, November 6, 2012.

- **The most complex and chaotic atmospheres are caused by other humans, rather than solely by environmental factors.** All of the professions operating in environments with high levels of chaos had humans as the primary generators of surprise. These surprises were not necessarily the result of a deliberate strategy, but reflected the unpredictability that results when many thinking, deciding humans interact.
- **When the surprise is caused by other humans, surprises are most likely to come from a third party, not the known adversary.** One of the key insights from our discussions with practitioners is that surprise is not as likely to come directly from an opponent; instead, the biggest challenges often come from third parties who may not even be key stakeholders. For example, the Navy SEAL told us he was surprised more often by domesticated animals than a direct adversary.[2]
- **Once a surprise occurs, practitioners' response depends more on whether the surprise is recognized or unrecognized than known versus unknown.** Our original hypothesis suggested a difference between KUs and UUs. We found that *recognized* versus *unrecognized* was a much more useful distinction, since practitioners' responses depended on whether the type of surprise was recognized or not when they had to decide on a response.

Operating in Contrived Environments

As our research progressed, so did our thinking about low-chaos environments. Our discussions with practitioners provided us with evidence that most low-chaos environments are also contrived environments.

The football field and improv theater are the most extreme examples of contrived environments. As we noted in the introduction, the NFL's playing field is literally defined by physical markers. Some football stadiums even have retractable roofs and climate control, further reducing the number of outside factors that can affect play. The improv

---

[2]   Interview with Navy SEAL team leader, November 6, 2012.

actor works on a well-defined stage, with the assumption that the actor will remain there, or at least inside the theater, and interact with the audience in a prescribed yet spontaneous way. The stage often employs lighting effects and curtains, both of which are designed to direct the audience's attention to what is happening on stage. In addition, both of these environments are maintained such that there is very little variation in the environment from day to day.

The nature of these environments also means that there is a specific set of rules that govern the interactions that can happen between the players and the spectators. Specifically, these environments are designed to limit the interactions between the participants using physical barriers and social norms. These limits help reduce the level of chaos in the environment, thereby containing the surprises to the ones that occur on the playing field. All of these factors contribute to a tightly controlled work environment. However, such literal "playing fields" are not just limited to the entertainment industry. As we have already discussed, a surgeon's operating room is also an example of a contrived environment, although certainly less so than the football field or theater stage. Operating rooms are heavily instrumented, climate controlled, well lit, and physical access is strictly controlled. Nurses and support staff also strive to measure and control as many factors as possible. Taken as a whole, all of these mechanisms serve to minimize chaos, reduce the number of possible surprises, and simplify the response when they do occur.

Contrived environments are also used by some professions in a more limited way, such as to plan responses to surprise. This is the case for the team at the Jet Propulsion Laboratory that operates the Mars rovers. When the rovers encounter trouble and the engineering team needs to test potential solutions, they use a duplicate rover that sits in a sandbox in Pasadena, California. This allows the engineers to test out new techniques and procedures as many times as necessary in a controlled environment, without worrying about making a potentially catastrophic move with the real rover on Mars. It also eliminates having to deal with any number of other variables, such as radio communication glitches, Martian weather, or the delay of up to 20 minutes that is imposed by transmitting commands hundreds of millions of miles to the actual rovers.[3]

In all of these examples, contrived environments serve to reduce the effect of outside factors on outcomes. In the case of the most contrived environments—like the playing field or theater stage—the outside factors have been reduced so much that there is a finite number of events that can happen on the field. In some cases, that number is small enough that it makes sense to develop a response plan for every possible scenario.

This is certainly the case within the NFL, where the experienced NFL coach has the luxury of devising a response plan for almost anything he is likely to encounter during a game. The result of this planning is the team's playbook, which is so extensive and specific that it represents a formulated response for any combination of opponent formation, down number, and field position. The playbook serves as a pre-planned response function: The inputs are formation, down number, and field position (yard line), and the output is the optimum play to execute in that situation.[4]

Given all this planning, there should not be any surprises during an NFL game. To hear the former coach describe the process, it sounded like a speed-chess match—another highly contrived environment—between two grandmasters, with move and countermove obvious at a glance. Indeed, the coach we spoke with had a hard time enumerating many situations when he was faced with any true UUs, which appears to be a credit to his experience and knowledge base.[5] (In the only example he was able to provide, the cause of the surprise was not a clever opponent, but a fluke of weather: A punt once landed *behind* the kicker in a blizzard, blown back by fierce winds.)

When asked, the coach was able to recall several examples of KUs, such as the opposing team executing a pass or rush on fourth down instead of attempting a field goal or punt, or their attempting to

---

[3]   Interview with Mars Rover personnel, November 15, 2012.

[4]   Interview with NFL coach, October 30, 2012.

[5]   Interview with NFL coach, October 30, 2012.

use an onside kick.[6] Both of these scenarios are recognized possibilities: Even when an opposing team executes one of those plays, the coaches and players were usually able to quickly identify the surprise, have a preplanned strategy in place, and execute an appropriate response.

Like the NFL coach, many other professions use a case-by-case breakdown to plan for KUs. One classic formulation of this approach is known as FMEA (failure modes and effects analysis). The idea is to systematically think through every possible way that a system could go wrong (the failure modes), what the consequences would be (effects), and what to do to prevent or respond to such failures (McDermott, Mikulak, and Beauregard, 2008). Variations of FMEA are used by many disciplines to improve quality and outcomes, including the fields of engineering, manufacturing, and medicine. This is an extension of Klein's RPD model—in these surprise settings, recognition and response is not just based on training and experience, but also on deep preparatory thought and planning.

The lesson we learned from the NFL coach was clear: To the extent that a surprise practitioner has the luxury and ability to envision a nearly complete set of the surprises that can occur, it makes sense to develop "what if" responses for most or all of them. Doing so significantly reduces the chance of being surprised, and it greatly facilitates a timely and appropriate response, increasing the probability of overall mission success.

Modulating Merely Moderate Chaos

In the previous section, we discussed how practitioners who operate in highly contrived environments can (and should) prepare for and respond to surprise. But what about those professionals who work in less-contrived or moderately chaotic environments? How does the approach of the Mars rover team, emergency room physician, or civil engineer differ from that of the NFL coach? The simple answer to this question is that since these practitioners deal with a larger set of poten-

---

[6]   Interview with NFL coach, October 30, 2012.

tial surprises, it does not make sense to do contingency planning for every possible outcome. Instead, they rely on a combination of pre-planned responses and more-generalized, all-purpose protocols.

Everyone we spoke with who works in a moderately chaotic environment—the middle row of practitioners in Figure 4.1 in Chapter Four: the public works engineer, the Mars rover operators, the emergency room physician, the test pilot, and the heart surgeon—can control that environment to some degree. Like the NFL coach, their goal is to reduce the size of the surprise space, shifting as many surprises as reasonably possible into the realm of having a specific plan. However, since these practitioners experience higher levels of chaos in their work environment, a larger number of things can go wrong. This implies that it will be impractical to prepare a contingency plan for every possible surprise. Several practitioners operating in more chaotic environments also noted that performing a mission or task that has never been done before usually has a much bigger surprise space, including many UUs, which are more challenging to mitigate via preplanning.

According to our interviews, all of these moderate chaos-level occupations address surprises by combining some degree of premeditation and planning with a set of general protocols or other best-practice recipes that prescribe how to respond in unforeseen or uncertain situations. For example, the public works engineer has an overall build plan with complete blueprints and specifications to ensure that the project meets the designer's intent. However, he also prepares a list of the most likely complications that may arise during construction and develops a mitigation plan for dealing with them. The public works engineer we spoke with noted that digging a foundation is always full of uncertainty. The planning team can take soil samples across the area, but there is no way to know for sure that the samples will be representative of the entire area. To account for this, he draws up mitigation plans that outline how the construction project will make adjustments if they find something unexpected while digging.[7] This form of preplanning is an effective strategy because if one of these more likely surprises occurs,

---

[7]   Interview with public works engineer, October 30, 2012.

he already will have done the front-end engineering needed to respond efficiently.

Both the pilot and the surgeon also rely on premeditation or visualization exercises, both alone and with their entire team, to help get everyone aligned to the upcoming mission or operation. Test pilots call this a safety conference. Surgeons refer to their conference as a "time out." Both practitioners noted that these exercises are beneficial because visualizing what is expected to happen and what could go wrong improves their ability to detect and respond when a surprise occurs or something otherwise does start to go wrong.[8]

Both the test pilot and the medical practitioners also rely heavily on protocols and premeditated procedures. The test pilot has a flight plan, checklists, and flight rules to minimize the chances something will go wrong by ensuring that steps are followed in the proper order. Checklists, also used by surgeons, are mostly designed to prevent people from forgetting to do something. Such errors of omission might include forgetting to trim the flaps before landing or neglecting to remove all of the surgical sponges from the patient before closing the incision.

In contrast to checklists, rules are mostly intended to prevent practitioners from taking some dangerous action. Rules form the boundary conditions for safe operations as a way to prevent fatal errors of commission. For example, the test pilot told us flight rules are "written in blood."[9] When, despite these flight rules, a potentially catastrophic surprise does occur, the pilot consults another set of protocols, carried inside the cockpit, that describe step by step what should be done in response to the most common shocks, such as an engine failure or an electrical fault.

The operators of the Mars rovers apply a similar strategy, but the special conditions of their operating environment necessitate an additional step. Mars is so far from Earth that it takes radio signals traveling at the speed of light up to 20 minutes to traverse the dis-

---

[8] Interview with chief of thoracic surgery, October 25, 2012; interview with test pilot, October 24, 2012.

[9] Interview with test pilot, October 24, 2012.

tance between the planets. If something catastrophic were to happen to a rover on Mars, it could take 20 minutes for scientists on Earth to first learn about it, and another 20 minutes for any Earth-based commands to travel back to the rovers in response. Because of this potential 40-minute delay, JPL has programmed the rovers with predetermined response plans for existential threats.[10]

For example, the movable communications dish on the top of the rovers must remain pointed at the Earth in order to maintain its connection with the JPL control team. If this dish were to accidentally start pointing elsewhere (for example, toward the Martian surface), the rovers would not be able to send and receive commands. Without further action, this scenario might mean the end of the mission because the rovers would continue to sit and wait forever, never receiving any further instructions. To prevent this situation, the rovers are preconfigured with an automated sequence that dictates what they should do to reestablish communications if the signal is lost. Those commands are executed automatically, preventing anomalies like a misaligned antenna from prematurely terminating the mission.[11]

As we have already noted, practitioners in moderately chaotic environments cannot preplan for every contingency because their set of potential surprises is too diverse. When tactical practitioners (SWAT captain, Navy SEAL, emergency room doctor, heart surgeon, and test pilot) encounter a situation they have not preplanned for, we were intrigued to learn that all of them described a nearly identical three-step protocol that they used when such an unanticipated or unrecognized surprise occurs: Control panic, buy time, and revert to fundamentals learned in training (see Figure 7.1). While the details and specific fundamentals differ by profession, they all have a similar flavor.

One practitioner who takes this approach is the emergency room physician, who goes back to the "ABCS" when faced with an unresponsive patient: Make sure the patient has an open *airway*; check their

---

[10] Interview with Mars Rover personnel, November 15, 2012.

[11] Interview with Mars Rover personnel, November 15, 2012.

Figure 7.1
Approaches for Dealing with Surprise in Moderately Chaotic Environments

Many practitioners performed active scanning for pre-imagined scenarios.

When an unanticipated surprise arises, the default strategy appears to have three key components.

RAND RR341-7.1

breathing; ensure effective blood *circulation*; and finally, treat them for *shock*.[12]

Pilots, when confronted with a sudden navigation hazard or threat, employ a similar strategy, encapsulated by the phrase "aviate, navigate, communicate."[13] The first step when responding to a shock event is to aviate: i.e., fly the plane and avoid immediate disaster. Next, navigate to safety using an appropriate escape maneuver. Finally, communicate with team members to alert them to the situation and plan a further response.

The approaches that we highlight here are very different from the one we constructed for our initial model. Before we conducted our discussions with practitioners, our initial model broke the process into four steps: recognizing that a surprise was occurring, gathering data, formulating a response, and executing it. Actual practitioners in the tactical professions taught us that in their realm, none of these actions was really essential. When faced with an unfamiliar, potentially mission- or life-threatening surprise, the proper response minimized the importance of thinking or planning, and instead emphasized the need to take nearly immediate action based on a general-purpose strategy they learned in training.

---

[12] Interview with emergency department physician, October 22, 2012.

[13] Interview with test pilot, October 24, 2012.

Such a general-purpose, preplanned strategy differs somewhat from Klein's RPD model. In that model, if a situation appears unfamiliar, the model suggests that practitioners try to match it to a typical and familiar scenario—or, failing that, simulate the outcomes of various response options to help pick the best one. Our investigation suggests that in unfamiliar tactical situations, there is often no time to perform those steps. Instead, practitioners almost immediately default to a generic response protocol.

The key lesson from this finding is that while it pays to preplan for as many scenarios as reasonably possible, the return on investment decreases as the complexity of the operating environment increases. In more-chaotic environments, practitioners should only do comprehensive planning for surprises that are either highly likely or represent existential threats. The opportunity cost of prethinking such scenarios is generally much lower than the cost of not having a plan, since having no plan might, for example, result in crashing the plane or killing the patient. However, it does not make sense to develop detailed plans for the many remaining surprises, which are less probable and less grave because that problem set is too large. Instead, practitioners develop and rely on a general-response framework, which helps them address these varied problems. We will discuss this idea in more detail in the next section.

Working in Highly Chaotic Environments

Practitioners such as CEOs, diplomats, and military personnel all work in what we characterize as highly chaotic environments, in which multiple factors interact and contribute to an extremely complex and unpredictable workplace. In general, we found that practitioners working in the most chaotic environments do not invest in the same high levels of specific response planning done by professionals in less-chaotic environments, and the reason is obvious: There are simply too many ways in which events can go wrong. Instead, when responding to surprise, all of the practitioners we spoke to who operate in highly chaotic environments rely on a general framework of initial responses designed to facilitate later action while still retaining flexibility.

Being the ambassador of a large U.S. embassy on foreign soil is a complex job. The practitioner we spoke with compared it to acting as the CEO of U.S.A. Incorporated, where he played the role of chief executive, data analyst, public relations specialist, and landlord.[14] As this former diplomat noted, a typical career with the State Department should not include many unexpected surprises, so he did not spend much time preparing for such events. In fact, there was a very large set of *potential* surprises, but all of them are individually unlikely. So while a few surprises are bound to occur across a long career in the Foreign Service, it is a waste of effort to develop a response plan in advance for them all.

However, the ambassador did spend time developing a general-response framework that he could rely on in case of an unexpected event. He referred to his framework as a "task force" and noted that it was the standard tool he used whenever he encountered a surprise. Therefore, he and his staff worked out the details of assembling a task force ahead of time. While they did not know what the specific surprise was going to be, they knew it would require office space, lines of communication, and the support of some key people inside and outside the embassy. They then prepared and practiced a process for quickly deploying this infrastructure when needed.[15]

The CEOs and Air Force general used a similar staff model for dealing with surprise.[16] Several of the practitioners we spoke with, principally those working in highly chaotic environments, summed up this approach by sharing an identical quote, attributed to Dwight D. Eisenhower: "Plans are nothing; planning is everything" (Office of the Federal Register, National Archives and Records Service, 1957, p. 818).

---

[14] Interview with U.S. ambassador, November 7, 2012.

[15] Interview with U.S. ambassador, November 7, 2012.

[16] Interview with U.S. Air Force general officer, November 9, 2012; interview with small-business CEO, November 7, 2012; interview with CEO of a firm with 1,200 worldwide employees, November 8, 2012.

Humans Magnify Chaos

In the course of talking with practitioners working in highly chaotic environments, we experienced a key insight: Everyone in the high-chaos space—the CEO, Foreign Service officer and ambassador, Air Force general officer, SWAT team captain, and Navy SEAL—faces surprises that are generated *by other humans.* This key fact is what distinguishes these practitioners from those shown in the more-moderate environments in Figure 4.1 in Chapter Four.

Humans think, plan, and decide, but their actions are often unpredictable, especially when a large number of people interact with one another. Many of these actions or decisions are likely not directed at a particular person, or intended with malice. For example, no one set out to purposely surprise CEOs with the collapse of the housing bubble and subsequent "Great Recession" in late 2008. When people are at the root of a surprise (as opposed to, say, the environment), the system becomes more complex and the outcome becomes more unpredictable. As a result, this dramatically magnifies the difficulty in developing specific response plans ahead of time.

In contrast to this are the practitioners who work in a moderate level of complexity and who usually face surprises caused by their environment, not other humans. For example, the operators of the Mars rovers, test pilots, and surgeons all face surprises created by natural forces.[17] The operators of the Mars rovers literally face environmental threats in the form of dust storms as the rovers move about on Mars. The thoracic surgeon faces the patient's physiology, and the test pilot faces his plane's mechanics, aerodynamics, and the atmosphere.

We found that the practitioners who face human-induced chaos prepare for surprise using a different, less premeditated method than the NFL coach or the test pilot. As we indicated above, all of the practitioners we spoke with who face surprises created by other humans rarely develop specific "what if" plans because there are simply too many scenarios to plan for. Instead, the professions featuring highly chaotic environments

---

[17] Several natural forces may interact with one another to generate more complex phenomena, but even this effect will generally produce a less chaotic environment than one dominated by human activity.

focus more on developing general response processes and equipping their team with flexible tools that can be used once the surprise occurs.

Surprise Generated by Third-Party Humans

If the most-complex environments are caused by human activity, and therefore the practitioners in these environments can not afford to make detailed response plans for every possible scenario, what about the improv actor or the NFL coach? How is it that their environments feature such low chaos, if their surprises are generated by other humans? To address this question, we will return to our discussion with the Navy SEAL.[18]

When a SEAL platoon goes out on a foot patrol, a lot can go wrong. SEALs are trained to recognize that many factors besides the adversary can influence a mission. When we asked the SEAL what factors are most likely to cause surprise on a foot patrol, his answer was unexpected: geese and civilians. Geese are both loud and territorial; both these characteristics pose a challenge when a SEAL platoon on the ground is trying to "move smoothly to move quickly."[19] Civilians pose an even larger challenge, because SEALs often have no way to predict their movement or intentions.

These observations led us to an important insight: The biggest surprises often come from third-party actors. Geese and civilians pose a major concern to the SEAL team because, unlike an adversary, the SEALs are less able to predict when they will encounter animals or civilians, or how those third parties will behave when encountered.

The best example he offered involved a night patrol when his team encountered a couple amorously engaged in the dark. From the SEAL's perspective, this scenario was problematic because there were so many

---

[18] Interview with Navy SEAL team leader, November 6, 2012.

[19] Interview with Navy SEAL team leader, November 6, 2012.

unknowns. Who were these people? How would they react if they discovered the SEALs? What was his team's best response?[20]

Before a mission, SEALs spend a lot of time thinking about their mission objective; consequently, they also spend a lot of time thinking about their adversary. What is the opponent's objective? How is the opponent likely to behave if they discover the SEALs? From the SEALs' perspective, these questions are much easier to address (and prepare for) than what to do if the platoon stumbles across a flock of geese or young lovers that could reveal their presence while on a foot patrol.

Armed with this insight, we can now also address why the NFL coach and improv actor—two occupations that both face surprises generated by other humans—nevertheless work in settings that we consider to be low-chaos. There are two contradictory processes at work: While these professions do face surprises usually generated by other humans, they also work in very structured environments that constrain decisions and actions. In addition, there are no third parties in NFL football or improvisational theater (save for the spectators). Thus, while unconstrained humans seem able to generate highly chaotic surprise environments, the constraints of a structured environment and paucity of third-party actors cancel this factor out. The end result is that these professionals employ some techniques used by other tacticians and some otherwise used only by strategists.

Recognized and Unrecognized Surprises

The practitioners in more-chaotic environments also taught us another lesson about surprise. Their experience revealed that dividing surprises into KUs and UUs was not the most relevant distinction.

Virtually all of the professionals we spoke with were familiar with the concept of KUs versus UUs, and many used them as part of their mental toolkit. We were therefore somewhat surprised to learn that

---

[20] In this case, the SEAL instructed his team to keep quiet and avoid an encounter because it only would have complicated their mission.

that division did not seem to resonate as much as we had expected; instead, a more useful dichotomy appears to be between a recognized situation and an unrecognized one.

When a surprise occurs, if it is clear what is happening (i.e., the situation is recognized), then an appropriate response will usually also become clear to the practitioner (either a specific plan worked out in advance, or the appropriate general response strategy). An unrecognized situation may be due to a UU, or it may represent a KU that has not yet been identified. In either case, while the situation remains unrecognized, the only available option is to revert to a basic response strategy until additional information is acquired and the situation becomes clearer.

For example, when we asked the SWAT team commander to describe a surprise that, at the time, represented a UU, he described a hostage situation during which male suspects had barricaded themselves in a house. After he and his team arrived on scene, several people in dresses came out the front door—too many people. Were they male and female hostages escaping, the suspects, or both? While this was certainly a new scenario to him (he had never seen suspects try this particular ploy before), the more important issue was that it was difficult to respond definitively until the situation clarified. He had to improvise a strategy to control this unrecognized surprise situation and resolve it into a recognizable one. He did this by gathering additional data in order to map his experience onto something recognizable so that he could start developing a response plan.

These observations also reinforce Klein's RPD model. He, too, highlighted the difference in response strategies when dealing with a recognized versus unrecognized surprise. There are two primary differences between his conclusions and ours. First, for recognized surprises, our practitioners emphasized a much greater role for previsualizing and preplanning specific responses, not just recognizing the proper response from experience. Second, for unrecognized or UU surprises, our practitioners emphasized a much greater role for an immediate preplanned generic response, rather than first parsing the situation, or tailoring a response to the circumstances.

Detecting a surprise and recognizing the actual situation can be difficult when facing a large potential surprise space and many distracting background events. Yet this is exactly the sort of surprise situation that practitioners in higher-chaos environments routinely encounter. We propose that this is not only why practitioners spend so much effort reducing chaos and filling in missing information before a surprise occurs, but also represents a key reason why they appear to rely primarily on basic planning and fundamental strategies to respond once one does.

Another aspect of unrecognized situations became clear when we asked surprise practitioners whether it was ever useful to delay any response and allow the situation to clarify as events took their course—what physicians call "watchful waiting." Essentially, none of them thought that this was a useful approach, although one strategic practitioner commented dismissively that, "That may be true in the political sphere." Their unanimity was striking, although this may also illustrate what behavioral psychologists refer to as the commission (i.e. pro-action) bias (Groopman, 2007): When confronted with an ambiguous choice between action and inaction, the majority prefers doing over waiting.

A final variation on the unrecognized situation, which we did not have time to explore with our participants in depth, is the so-called unknown known. This is the surprise situation that occurs when a practitioner believes he or she recognizes what is going on, but in fact has misidentified the true state of affairs. In this case, they are likely to select the wrong response option—or rather, the right response option for the wrong situation. A quote often misattributed to Mark Twain puts it most succinctly: "It ain't what you don't know that gets you into trouble. It's what you know for sure that just ain't so" (Keyes, 2006).[21]

---

[21] Keyes credits this to humorist Josh Billings (whose real name was Henry Wheeler Shaw).

CHAPTER EIGHT

How Do Strategists Differ from Tacticians in Dealing with Surprise?

According to our initial hypothesis, shown in Figure 4.1 in Chapter Four, practitioners can be sorted into two classes, depending on how much time they typically have available when responding to a surprise. Up to this point, we have highlighted the similarities in how both strategists and tacticians respond to surprise. However, we learned that the available response time does indeed affect how practitioners prepare for and respond to surprise. Overall, we observed several differences between the strategists and the tacticians:

- **Strategists have to work harder at identifying and reacting to surprise.** Communication and coordination are key elements for both strategic and tactical professions, but these elements are required more often and earlier in the response process for strategists. The strategic practitioners—those who generally must react within hours and days instead of seconds or minutes—have to rely more on others to detect and identify surprises. They also rely even more on teamwork than tacticians when responding to surprise.
- **Strategists use a different response loop than tacticians.** Due to the nature of their work, strategists often have to coordinate larger numbers of people and resources, which means they use a different response loop than the tacticians do.

Throughout our discussions, teamwork was a common topic; nearly everyone cited it as an important element when dealing with surprise. Specifically, practitioners noted that communication and coordination were key processes for minimizing surprises and their consequences, even for the seemingly "solo" practitioners, such as test pilots.

We also made an (intuitive) observation that top-level strategists are usually not the first people in the organization to observe or detect a surprise. Instead, they usually rely on other team members to monitor for surprises, after which any indications and messages must work their way through an organizational hierarchy to reach the primary decisionmaker. Tactical professions may also rely on other team members to detect surprises, but tacticians are—by definition—usually closer to the action and therefore are in a position to respond more quickly. The result of this distinction is that strategists must expend more effort on communication and coordination than tacticians to detect surprises promptly and reliably.

Given the generally larger organizational scale that accompanies their longer time frame, CEOs, diplomats, and civil engineers have both the luxury and the necessity of coordinating more personnel when responding to surprise. Their response often requires significant input or action by other team members, and therefore significant communication and coordination. The fact that strategists must communicate and coordinate more in order to detect and identify a surprise is likely just one consequence of the need to coordinate so many people as compared to tacticians.

We also observed that strategists use a different response loop than the tactical professions. While quite different from that used by tacticians, the loop was quite similar among the different strategic professions:

1. **Control emotion.** The first step is to control emotion. While this concept is superficially the same as the tacticians' first step (control panic), most of the strategists that we spoke with noted that they were most often angry right after being surprised. In addition, they noted that they had to work hard at not taking the surprise personally and overreacting. This differs from the tacticians, who more often were dealing with fear and anxiety.

We have already described how the CEO learned to resist the tendency to send off intemperate emails and deploy maximum force in responding to lawsuits. We heard another example from the public works engineer, who described how his team's first tendency when confronted by a surprise setback was to rely only on their own resources to resolve the issue instead of reaching to industry contacts for help. "We're the [State Transportation Agency]—we know how to do this!" Unless prompted to do otherwise, confidence in their own abilities kept them from consulting with outside experts on the problem.[1]

2. **Take initial enabling actions.** The second step is to take enabling actions; i.e., actions that will facilitate further response. Earlier we described how the Air Force general immediately put specific personnel on alert and other units into motion because he knew in advance that they would likely be needed soon, even though at that point the 9/11 attacks represented an unclear and dynamic situation.

3. **Assemble the staff to generate a plan.** The third step in the response loop is to assemble the staff of trusted advisers and decisionmakers, including anyone essential to evaluating the situation or planning the response. The ambassador and the CEOs all emphasized that they relied heavily on a core team of trusted co-workers whenever there was a crisis. The ambassador, in particular, noted that, as the "CEO of U.S. Incorporated, I cannot be everywhere at once when a crisis occurs. I rely heavily on a trusted core group of advisers, and I entrust my reputation [as ambassador] to them."[2]

4. **Institute the response.** As a final step, all of the strategic practitioners emphasized how essential it is that everyone on the staff worked in unison within the overall plan. Specifically, all of the strategists told us that their direct reports had to understand their specific roles when responding to a surprise, and the management team had to present the rest of the organization and

---

[1]   Interview with public works engineer, October 30, 2012.

[2]   Interview with U.S. ambassador, November 7, 2012;

outsiders with a consistent message as they put the response into action.

Together, these steps summarize a consistent response mechanism that we heard from all of the strategic practitioners, although (as stated before) these steps differ substantially from the tacticians who more often rely on preestablished response plans. They also differ from the Klein model, which was based more on observing tacticians.

Overall, the theme we heard from all of the strategists was that effective communication was critical, especially when trying to prevent cascading surprises. When we asked practitioners about their experiences with surprises that could cascade out of control, most of them attributed such events to failures in communication. The public works engineer used a major bridge refurbishment project as an example. In this project, some of the steel was sourced from a foreign mill. While this fact was known by everyone, what was not well communicated within the engineering team was how the foreign steel's specifications differed from those of domestic steel. As a result, the foreign steel was used in inappropriate components, which eventually required some major engineering repairs later on.[3] In another example, the heart surgeon described what happened when one subteam failed to communicate with the others regarding a drop in a patient's blood pressure. Unaware of the condition, the other subteams took actions that would otherwise be appropriate, but in this case made a fairly routine situation much worse. This created still more surprise issues, all of which then needed to be addressed at the same time.[4]

To summarize, we found that strategists respond to surprise using a different method than tacticians because strategists have to respond to a different set of motivating factors. They must cope with a more complex organizational structure, rely much more on communication and coordination, and overcome different emotional impediments when responding to surprise. In the next chapter, we will examine whether any of our participants viewed surprise as an opportunity.

---

[3]   Interview with public works engineer, October 30, 2012.

[4]   Interview with chief of thoracic surgery, October 25, 2012.

CHAPTER NINE

Surprise as an Opportunity

Until near the end of each discussion with our surprise practitioners, we never guided the conversation to suggest that surprises could be positive or negative. Therefore, it was interesting to observe that nearly everyone associated surprise with negative—or at least potentially harmful—outcomes. Toward the end of conversations, we asked the practitioners if they ever considered that surprises could represent positive opportunities. The responses to this question varied, but the discussions that followed yielded two insights:

- **Some surprises only yield direct benefits if you prepare in advance to take advantage of them.** Without preparation for these events, it is usually impossible to react quickly enough to enable a positive outcome. Alternatively, without some preplanning, other team members may be unprepared to respond.
- **Most surprises present an opportunity if approached with the proper mind-set.** Many surprises can be converted into an advantage only if recognized as such, most often by treating them as a learning opportunity.

Almost all surprise practitioners recognized that surprises can have positive implications but we observed two types of opportunity-laden surprises: Some require advance preparation; others require the correct approach.

The first type of surprise is one that represents obvious opportunities. Using this type of surprise to one's advantage is difficult not because they are difficult to recognize, but because circumstances can change quickly as events unfold and make the window of opportunity very narrow. This means that the surprise practitioner must act quickly, which often requires either specific advance preparations or knowing precisely the proper action to take when opportunity arises. In either case, the practitioners must be prepared to take advantage of the surprise.

The clearest example shared with us came from the test pilot. During the Vietnam War, U.S. pilots often reported encountering enemy aircraft unexpectedly and in situations that briefly allowed them an easy kill shot. Unfortunately, the pilots were rarely able to convert these surprise opportunities into actual kills because it took too long to activate their weapons systems. At the time, the weapons activation process required several steps that simply took too long. In response to this problem, the Air Force revised the weapons system in later generations of fighters to simplify activation, greatly improving the kill rate for such targets of opportunity.[1]

The cardiothoracic surgeon shared another example of how an inability to switch modes quickly enough may let opportunity pass.[2] He told us that he occasionally would begin a procedure only to discover that the surgical problem was much simpler than expected. This meant that he could complete the procedure in a shorter time, exposing the patient to less risk from anesthesia or the heart-lung bypass machine. He learned, however, that a key element in taking advantage of such opportunities was communicating the change in plans to the anesthesiologist and bypass specialists early. If he neglected to do so, then his part of the operation might still end quickly, but the patient derived much less benefit because of the time it takes to reverse those other interventions.

These two examples highlight an observation we made earlier: Surprises can often be turned into a positive outcome if appropriate preparations are made in advance. We were also curious to learn how often surprises might be converted into a positive outcome if the practitioner assumed a productive mind-set.

---

[1]   Interview with test pilot, October 24, 2012.

[2]   Interview with chief of thoracic surgery, October 25, 2012.

As it turned out, mind-set played a different role than we originally envisioned. Our initial model postulated that a surprise approach designed to constantly scan for threats might cause practitioners to miss surprises with positive implications. None of the practitioners felt that this was a significant problem in their discipline. Instead, they taught us that a surprise can be converted into an opportunity, and that the right response can channel even some surprises with negative implications into a positive result. The key to this is having the right approach, asking either, "How can I benefit from this scenario?" Or, alternatively, "What can we learn from it?"

The football coach provided one concrete example. He explained how an unexpected play by an opponent—especially a play that is unsuitable or unusual—can be converted into an advantage for his team. The key to leveraging this opportunity is to move past the surprise and ask, "How can we take advantage of this situation?" He trained his team to do just that, including developing the proper response to an array of unusual scenarios.[3] This example illustrates how a combination of preparation and mind-set can convert surprise into opportunity.

Several practitioners also suggested that nearly any surprise can be converted into an opportunity by viewing it as a learning occasion. The civil engineer shared a quite nuanced example of this: During a recent bridge refurbishment project, the team encountered an engineering setback and was forced to delay opening one deck of the bridge to traffic. They treated this setback not merely as a learning opportunity, but also as a chance to carefully reassess their current plans. Their subsequent reassessment revealed an unambiguously better approach. While there was still a delay in opening the level to traffic in the originally planned direction, they realized that once they resolved that delay, there was no reason not to open the deck to traffic in both directions at same time, much earlier than they had originally planned.[4]

---

[3]   Interview with NFL coach, October 30, 2012.

[4]   Interview with public works engineer, October 30, 2012.

CHAPTER TEN

Helpful Lessons from Specific Professions

In addition to all of the techniques described above, we observed two occupation-specific viewpoints that may provide additional help when responding to surprise:

- **Accept what has happened and build on it in a constructive manner.** The improv actor noted that the phrase "Yes, and…" is one of the fundamental tenets in improvisational theater.[1] This perspective is a useful lesson for dealing with surprise because it encourages the practitioner to accept what happened and focus their energy on moving forward instead of questioning why or rejecting the current reality.
- **Look outside immediate circles of influence for help and counsel.** We observed that more experience leads to fewer surprises. It follows from this that reaching outside the local context to other experienced professionals is an effective way to prepare for and respond to surprise.

Yes, and…

When improv actors start a scene, they are at the mercy of their fellow actors. For example, if the first actor walks on stage and starts setting a dinner table and the next actor enters the scene holding a pitchfork, suddenly the first actor appears to be setting a dinner table in hell and

---

[1] Interview with a improvisational theater instructor and performer, November 11, 2012.

is expected to behave accordingly. In improvisational theater, the circumstances are such that new details must be accepted by everyone on stage. The actors refer to this approach as "Yes, and…", and it is a fundamental tenet in improvisational performance. Another useful example is the practice of aikido, a martial art that focuses not on working against an opponent's energy, but rather channeling and directing it for your own benefit. An aikido practitioner will not merely block or deflect an incoming punch, they will augment their adversary's motion to pull them into a takedown, bind, or throw.

The "Yes, and…" approach is a useful framework for responding to surprise because it encourages the practitioner to move forward and not dwell on inessentials. When surprises occur, especially shocking surprises, many people's first instinct is to question or deny. How did this happen? Why me? How could this have been prevented? This can't be happening! As many of the practitioners we spoke with taught us, in the immediate aftermath of a shocking surprise, these responses are usually not the most useful or productive. Instead, practitioners should accept the fact that the surprise occurred and start developing ways to address the new reality. The "Yes, and…" mind-set is a perfect characterization of how to proceed immediately after a shock.

Look Outside the Immediate Network for Help

One of the practitioners we spoke with worked for a state government agency, and he noted that he was required by his state's legislation to look outside his organization for help when he encountered a delay on his project. This turned out to be a powerful innovation for two reasons. First, this mechanism required the engineering team to look past their overconfidence and go outside their immediate group for expertise offered by anyone in the world.[2] Second, as we have discussed earlier, this greatly expanded their experience base: When the whole world is available for consultation, there are likely very few surprises that do not already have a recognized solution. Taking this approach gave the

---

[2] Interview with public works engineer, October 30, 2012.

engineering team access to a larger knowledge base, which allowed them to respond to surprises more quickly and with better solutions.

CHAPTER ELEVEN

Key Observations and Their Implications

Our overall goal in conducting this research was to learn how different occupations respond to surprise so we could help identify ways that people (and organizations) could become more flexible and agile. We began by presenting a framework that allowed us to classify our set of professions by reaction time and level of chaos (Figure 4.1 in Chapter Four). We used this framework to develop a set of hypotheses that were primarily based on the belief that different classes of occupations (as characterized by our framework in Figure 4.1) will respond to surprise in different ways. We then tested our hypotheses by conducting informal discussions with surprise practitioners, and we found that most of our original hypotheses appear valid. We concluded that an effective framework to characterize surprise occupations is based on two key variables: typical response time and level of environmental chaos.

In this final section, we summarize our key findings and make some observations on their implications. We also propose some practical suggestions and reiterate others that practitioners can apply when confronting surprise.

Key Findings

One of the primary objectives of our research was to determine whether all of the occupations relied on a common set of strategies for dealing with surprise, and we did find a number of coping strategies that were common across all of the professions. Specifically, we found that all practitioners rely heavily on experience, since it is what gives practitioners the ability to map current circumstances onto something more familiar. We also observed that all professionals we interviewed try to reduce the level of chaos in the operating environment, thereby also reducing the complexity and size of the solution space, which then makes it easier to respond to surprises when they occur. We learned that it is best to react to surprises with a measured response to preserve further options as the surprise unfolds. Finally, we observed that teamwork plays an essential role when responding to unexpected events, even for those professions that we incorrectly perceived as relying on individual actors, such as heart surgeons or test pilots.

After comparing specific classes of professions, we made some additional observations on how different groups prepare for and respond to the unexpected. First, we observed that the level of environmental chaos encountered by each occupation strongly influences how practitioners in that occupation prepare for and respond to surprise. Specifically, we found that practitioners who work in the most contrived environments, such as athletic fields or theatrical stages, face only a finite range of events. Because of this, some of these practitioners are able to plan reactions for nearly any possible event, and practitioners in the NFL, for example, regularly do so. Practitioners who work in moderately chaotic environments such as operating rooms or cockpits rely partially on checklists and rules, but they also employ some basic response frameworks that they can fall back on if the surprise event is not covered by a more specific protocol. The most challenging circumstances are faced by those practitioners working in highly chaotic environments, such as a foreign embassy or behind enemy lines. Their environment is so complex and unpredictable that it does not make sense to do much planning against specific surprise events, unless those events are highly likely or represent an existential threat. Instead, practitioners working in highly chaotic environments develop and exercise a general-purpose framework (like the ambassador's "task force" mentioned earlier) that can be deployed whenever a major surprise is encountered.

The second characteristic that we tried to assess was whether the amount of response time affects the way that practitioners prepare for and respond to surprise events. We found that strategists—those who have hours or days to react to typical surprises—use a different approach than tacticians, people who must generally react within a few seconds or minutes. When tacticians are surprised, they have limited time to respond, and often must first overcome feelings of fear and anxiety. We found that most tacticians employ a similar protocol to counteract these emotions and then respond effectively using minimal analysis: specifically, they first employ mechanisms that control panic; next, ones that buy time; and finally, revert to fundamentals learned in training. By contrast, we observed that strategists often encounter a different set of emotions when surprised; they must control immediate feelings of anger, along with the impulse to overreact. To combat these feelings and respond effectively, all of the strategists that we spoke with employed essentially the same four step process: control emotions, take some initial enabling actions, quickly assemble key staffers, and disseminate a coherent longer-term response throughout the organization.

In addition to the key three conclusions described above, we, as investigators, found ourselves surprised by three findings that challenged our original model. The first was that most practitioners we spoke with do not think about surprises as KUs and UUs. Instead, it is most useful to think about two classes of surprise situations: recognized surprises and unrecognized surprises. We propose that practitioners and future researchers adopt these terms to categorize surprise events. These terms resonated much more with all of our participants than KUs and UUs. Second, we were surprised to discover that the most highly chaotic environments all feature surprises generated by other humans. Practitioners facing surprises initiated by another human, rather than environmental factors such as weather or other physical processes, normally operate in highly chaotic environments, which—as we noted above—often precludes engaging preplanned options. Instead, these practitioners focus on developing general, flexible response frameworks. Finally, we observed that for practitioners in the most-chaotic environments, surprises often arise from third parties' actions rather than from direct adversaries or stakeholders. The intuitive explanation for this is that practitioners usually have a good understanding of their most direct threats—they understand the motives and factors that drive adversary or stakeholder behavior and can make appropriate plans to avert surprise. However, those preparations still leave them open and vulnerable to less predictable third-party actions, even when that third party has no adversarial intent.

Finally, we observed that almost all surprises represent opportunities, given the proper mind-set and preparation. Surprises that present only brief opportunities usually require advanced preparation to capitalize on them. This may mean making changes to equipment, communications, or procedures to allow a sufficiently rapid response. It might also require anticipating or previsualizing your response to specific opportunities should they arise. Some surprises can be converted into opportunities by responding in an unexpected way. Finally, virtually every surprise can be used as a learning experience, either at the time or after the fact.

Implications and Suggested Practices Moving Forward

All of the observations presented above motivate the obvious question: How can someone become better at responding to surprise and develop greater skill at future planning? As we believe we have demonstrated, the answer to this question depends to some degree on occupation, although many strategies apply broadly to all.

As noted above, nearly everyone told us that nothing substitutes for experience, and we observed they were tacitly referring to two types of experience: individual and organizational. Practically speaking, this means organizations that are seeking to minimize surprise also need to attract and retain the most experienced people. In addition to all of the other benefits that come from hiring proficient personnel, experienced people may also represent an organization's best general defense against surprise.

Practitioners can take additional measures beyond emphasizing corporate and professional experience, including strengthening communications and coordination between co-workers, developing mechanisms and tools to promote more measured responses, and instilling their workforce with the mind-set that surprises can be both opportunities and learning experiences.

In addition to these suggestions aimed at all practitioners, our results also suggest some lessons targeted at specific classes of professionals. We found that strategists are often in charge of large groups of people or whole organizations, and therefore tend to be much more reliant on a staff and team approach to handle their logistically larger surprises. Top-level strategists often are not the first person in the organization to detect surprises when they occur, so they must have good communication with their co-workers throughout the entire response effort.

Based on our conversations, there are a few mechanisms strategists can employ to become better at detecting and responding to surprises. First, as both of the CEOs pointed out, an effective strategist is one who is not consumed in the day-to-day operations of their organization. It is certainly tempting for strategists to spend time on routine issues; they are, after all, master problem solvers, and daily operations present a target-rich environment of satisfyingly solvable problems. The lesson that we learned from the CEOs is that it requires considerable work and discipline to delegate management of daily operations to a subordinate and instead focus on the harder problem: constantly looking toward the horizon, trying to anticipate and detect surprises.[1]

Successful strategists should also develop a network of trusted colleagues at all levels of the organization. Beyond providing an effective response network during a surprise, they will also function as surprise sensors throughout the organization, greatly expanding the chief strategist's field of view. When surprises occur, they should also not hesitate to reach beyond this network and seek outside expertise when appropriate.

Our final practical lesson for strategists builds on the idea that most surprises are likely to come from third-party stakeholders. This observation means that strategists can gain significant benefit from conducting regular exercises designed to identify alternative futures. When conducting these exercises, strategists should instruct the participants to adopt an open perspective and a very wide field of view,

---

[1]   Interview with small-business CEO, November 7, 2012.; interview with CEO of a firm with 1,200 worldwide employees, November 8, 2012.

not focusing solely on known stakeholders, competitors, and adversaries, but also potential actions by third parties. While the goal should be to identify the largest set of possible threats, simply identifying all potential sources of surprise represents an important first step toward mitigating possible surprise effects.

Based on our interviews, we observed a similar set of lessons for the tacticians. For this group, the first step in becoming more effective at responding to surprise should be to assess the level of chaos in their work environments. Those who work in more-contrived environments should spend most of their energy developing comprehensive response plans for each of the threats they expect to encounter. Those practitioners working in moderately or highly chaotic environments should develop specific response plans primarily for their most likely surprises *and* for existential threats. They should also develop and exercise more generalized response frameworks for whenever an unanticipated or an *unrecognized* surprise occurs. Those frameworks should also encourage a forward-moving, "yes, and…" response to surprise.

Like the strategists, tacticians can also benefit from the observation that many surprises come from third parties. While most tacticians probably do not engage in formal exercises designed to identify alternative future scenarios, they can benefit from the approach associated with those events. To that end, tacticians should spend part of their planning time specifically thinking about threats or surprises that could originate from outside their usual field of view. It may be helpful to engage a third party in this exercise to further expand the scope. That expanded scope should also encompass surprises that represent potential opportunities, and the exercise should consider any advance preparations needed to capitalize on them.

In Conclusion

This research allowed us to connect with a diverse array of talented, dedicated professionals, all of whom have devoted considerable thought and effort to developing their approach toward surprise. As with most other professional activities, coping with surprise is a learned skill. Acquiring experience is one aspect because it develops better surprise intuition. However, experience is only one of the components needed for success: Practitioners also employ well-tested protocols and methods. Many of these methods represent other practitioners' hard-learned lessons, "rules written in blood." Fortunately, protocols apply at any level of experience, and they can be learned and implemented immediately.

When we first started researching the idea of occupational surprise, we never expected that this work would yield so many practical insights. However, now that the research is complete, our hope is that others will be able to use these results in identifying lessons to employ in their own surprise situations. As we have demonstrated, there is compelling evidence to suggest that a Navy SEAL can learn a lot from a CEO (and vice versa). As the old saying goes: Wise men learn by other men's mistakes, fools by their own.

Bibliography

Baiocchi, Dave, and William Welser IV, *Confronting Space Debris: Strategies and Warnings from Comparable Examples Including Deepwater Horizon*, Santa Monica, Calif.: RAND Corporation, MG-1042-DARPA, 2010. As of June 11, 2013: http://www.rand.org/pubs/monographs/MG1042.html

Bazerman, Max H., and Michael D. Watkins, *Predictable Surprises: The Disasters You Should Have Seen Coming, And How to Prevent Them*, Harvard Business School Publishing Corporation, 2008.

Fischhoff, B., S. Lichtenstein, P. Slovic, S. L. Derby, and R. L. Keeney, *Acceptable Risk*, New York: Cambridge University Press, 1981.

Groopman, Jerome E., and Michael Prichard, *How Doctors Think*, Boston, Mass.: Houghton Mifflin, 2007.

Keyes, Ralph, *The Quote Verifier: Who Said What, Where and How*, New York: Ralph Keyes, 2006.

Klein, Gary A., *Sources of Power: How People Make Decisions*, MIT Press, 1998.

Klein, Gary, *The Power of Intuition: How to Use Your Gut Feelings to Make Better Decisions at Work*, Crown Business, 2007.

McCall, Morgan W., Michael M. Lombardo, and Ann M. Morrison, *Lessons of Experience: How Successful Executives Develop on the Job*, Free Press, 1988.

McDermott, R. E., R. J. Mikulak, and M. R. Beauregard, *The Basics of FMEA*, Productivity Press, 2008.

Mitchell, Melanie, *Complexity: A Guided Tour*, Oxford University Press, 2009.

Morgan, M. G., "Choosing and Managing Technology-Induced Risk," *IEEE Spectrum*, Vol. 18, No. 12, 1981.

Myers, Harold B., "For Lockheed, Everything's Coming Up Unk-Unks," *Fortune*, August 1969.

Neustadt, Richard E., and Ernest R. May, *Thinking in Time: The Uses of History for Decision Makers*, Free Press, 1986.

Office of the Federal Register, National Archives and Records Service, *Public Papers of the Presidents of the United States*, Washington, D.C., 1957.

Pasteur, Louis, "Discours Prononcé à Douai, le 7 Décembre 1854, à l'Occasion de l'Installation Solennelle de la Faculté des Lettres de Douai et de la Faculté des Sciences de Lille (Inauguration to the Faculty of Letters of Douai and the Faculty of Sciences of Lille)," December 7, 1854, reprinted in Vallery-Radot, Pasteur, ed., *Oeuvres de Pasteur*, Paris, France: Masson and Co., 1939.

Seely, Hart, *Pieces of Intelligence: The Existential Poetry of Donald H. Rumsfeld*, New York: Free Press, 2003.

Taleb, Nassim Nicholas, *The Black Swan: The Impact of the Highly Improbable*, Random House, 2007.

Watkins, Michael D., and Max H. Bazerman, "Predictable Surprises: The Disasters You Should Have Seen Coming," *Harvard Business Review*, Vol. 81, No. 3, 2003.

Weick, Karl E., and Kathleen M. Sutcliffe, *Managing the Unexpected: Resilience Performance in an Age of Uncertainty, (2nd Ed)*, San Francisco: Jossey-Bass, 2007.

Weiss, Robert S., *Learning from Strangers: The Art and Method of Qualitative Interview Studies*, Free Press, 2008.

Willis, Henry H., Andrew R. Morral, Terrence K. Kelly, and Jamison Jo Medby, *Estimating Terrorism Risk*, Santa Monica, Calif.: RAND Corporation, MG-388-RC, 2005. As of August 16, 2010: http://www.rand.org/pubs/monographs/MG388.html

Wolfe, Tom, *The Right Stuff*, New York: Farrar, Straus, Giroux, 1983.